Confronting Evil in Our Time

A Christian Devotional Inspired by C. S. Lewis's The Screwtape Letters

Written by
Ian Faith and Galen Balinski

Confronting Evil in Our Time
A Christian Devotional Inspired by C. S. Lewis's The Screwtape Letters
Written by Ian Faith and Galen Balinski
© 2025 Global Creative Group, LLC – First Edition – All Rights Reserved

ISBN: 9798994972502

Contents

This book is dedicated to Charlie Kirk, a man who gave his life standing up for his faith. His courage was matched by kindness, his conviction by love. His example and tenacity have influenced countless lives and stirred the hearts of millions. May his legacy inspire us to live boldly, love deeply, and fight for what is good.

"Courage is not simply one of the virtues, but the form of every virtue at the testing point."

\- C. S. Lewis

"Our Father, who art in Heaven, hallowed be thy name.

Thy kingdom come, thy will be done, on earth as it is in Heaven.

Give us this day our daily bread and forgive us our trespasses,

as we forgive those who trespass against us,

Lead us not into temptation but deliver us from the evil one."

Yes, the EVIL one.

Preface: Our Aspiration for This Work

This book was born out of a conviction and a calling. It began as a podcast, a journey through C. S. Lewis's *The Screwtape Letters*, and grew into something deeper: a shared mission to help people see the reality of spiritual warfare in our day. We are living in a time when truth is contested, when good and evil often trade names, and when courage and conviction are desperately needed among God's people.

Spiritual warfare is not a distant or dramatic idea. It is the quiet and constant battle for the soul that takes place in our hearts, our homes, and our culture. It is fought in the choices we make, the truths we defend, and the ways we love and serve others. Our desire is to help readers recognize that battle and step into it with wisdom and strength. Our aim is not to provoke or to posture, but to stand with courage, to speak truth in love and equip believers to discern the times. We believe that while evil may take new forms in each generation, the underlying battle remains the same. The same lies, fears, and temptations that Lewis described decades ago still operate today, though they now bear modern forms and emphases.

This book is our humble effort to expose those lies, illuminate the strategies of the enemy, and strengthen believers to walk wisely in a world that desperately needs light. We write as fellow soldiers, not generals. Our intent is not to pick fights, but to stand firm where God has placed us. Jesus declared that all authority in heaven and on earth belongs to Him, and our calling is to stand in that authority with wisdom, clarity, and love. We seek to help readers do the same.

Ian Faith was raised in the United Kingdom within the Catholic and Church of England traditions, experiences that gave him an appreciation for the historic church while grounding his present convictions in a Bible-believing, non-denominational faith. He brings a professional background in the music industry and executive-level marketing, offering insight into the cultural and professional systems that shape the modern world. Galen Balinski was raised attending Baptist churches and came to know the Lord at a young age. He was ordained as a pastor in New York City and later served in a thriving church in Arizona, where he and Ian met. His background in biblical studies, theology, and pastoral ministry provides a foundation for this work.

Though our paths have been different, we now stand united in our faith and commitment to Jesus Christ and Scripture. Our desire is to offer a resource that blends heart, reason, and faith that calls believers to courage and wisdom. It is our aspiration that these pages inspire you to live boldly, love truthfully, and confront evil in our time.

Introduction: What This Book Is and Isn't

This book is written by two authors. Throughout these pages, you will hear both of our voices. At times, we speak collectively as "we," and at other times one of us may speak in the first person to share a personal experience or insight. In these moments, we do not feel the need to identify which author is speaking as our purpose is not to draw attention to ourselves, but rather to the truth we hope to illuminate.

Confronting Evil in Our Time is a devotional cultural commentary inspired by C. S. Lewis's *The Screwtape Letters*. It uses the timeless insights of Lewis's work as a springboard to explore how the same spiritual principles apply in our modern world. Each chapter corresponds to one of the thirty-one letters written by Lewis, expanding on central ideas that speak to the nature of demonic temptation, faith, and human nature. These ideas are revisited through Scripture, prayer, and reflection, bringing contemporary relevance and practical wisdom.

This is not a companion guide or critique of *The Screwtape Letters*. It is not an academic analysis or a derivative work. It is a cultural commentary that is devotional in nature, designed to edify and equip Christians in our day. Our goal is to help believers see the world more clearly, resist the schemes of the enemy, and live with courage and discernment. Some chapters follow the structure of Lewis's letters closely, while others take more creative paths, expanding ideas to apply them more pointedly to our time. Yet all are written to help you understand the spiritual realities of life through the lens of faith and truth.

We invite you to read this book as you would a devotional, a Christian self-help guide, or a field manual for your spiritual war. It is written to stir the heart, strengthen faith, and help believers walk wisely in the world. May these pages encourage you to discern the times, stand firm in Christ, and confront evil with steadfastness and truth.

All truth is God's truth.

Chapter 1
Distraction, Fuddlement, and Jargon

For readers who have never read C. S. Lewis's *The Screwtape Letters*, allow us to give a brief explanation so you can better understand this book. Lewis's classic consists of thirty-one letters written by Screwtape, a senior demon, to his apprentice nephew, Wormwood. Through these letters, Screwtape advises and rebukes Wormwood on how to tempt and deceive a young man known only as "the patient." The story unfolds as a window into the unseen spiritual struggle for every human soul. While not inspired like Scripture, the book is uniquely and profoundly insightful. It presents demonic strategy, scriptural truth, and spiritual insight, revealing how Satan seeks to draw people away from God. Until you can read Lewis's book for yourself (and we HIGHLY recommend you do), this summary will help you appreciate the context behind the ideas we explore.

When most of us think about "spiritual warfare" or "demonic attack," we tend to visualize scenes from horror movies like The Exorcist or The Omen, people possessed by demons, displaying terrifying, grotesque contortions. We dismiss it as fiction and stop taking spiritual warfare seriously. As C. S. Lewis warns in the opening of The Screwtape Letters, to think too much or too little of the devil is what makes us vulnerable, and he is pleased with either extreme. Demonic forces operate their spiritual warfare on humanity with relentless intent, sabotaging us by weaponizing the ordinary, mundane moments of life, creating distractions like materialism, busyness, and noise to dull spiritual awareness.

Through these letters, we will explore a multitude of strategies and tactics used by the demonic and provide Scripture and wisdom to repel the attacks. If you think you are free from these assaults simply because you are a Christian, think again. Even Christ Himself was directly tempted by the Devil. We must remain vigilant against daily assaults that seek to mute deeper truths and divert life's focus from what truly matters, Christ. One strategy, known as "fuddling," is akin to intoxication; the same way alcohol can have the effect of dulling the senses, leading to a hazy frame of mind. Satan's goal is often to desensitize us to the important things in life by keeping us preoccupied with the mundane, the unnecessary, or just flat-out lies. Modern snares such as endless social media scrolling, excessive screen time, and more are all examples of vices designed to drown out moments of reflection. Attacks infiltrate our minds to keep our thoughts and perspectives shallow and misdirected. If we are not fuddled or distracted, they use "jargon" to confuse biblical truth. Satan knows the game, and he plays it well.

Scripture

"Now the serpent was more cunning than any beast of the field which the Lord God had made. And he said to the woman, "Has God indeed said, 'You shall not eat of every tree of the garden'?" And the woman said to the serpent, "We may eat the fruit of the trees of the garden; but of the fruit of the tree which is in the midst of the garden, God has said, 'You shall not eat it, nor shall you touch it, lest you die.'" Then the serpent said to the woman, "You will not surely die. For God knows that in the day you eat of it your eyes will be opened, and you will be like God, knowing good and evil." So when the

woman saw that the tree was good for food, that it was pleasant to the eyes, and a tree desirable to make one wise, she took of its fruit and ate. She also gave to her husband with her, and he ate." - Genesis 3:1-6

Distraction

Distraction is the first of three themes we find in Letter 1.

In life, we're guaranteed to get older, but not necessarily wiser. Wisdom is something we have to actively seek and ask for. If we go through life without contemplation and deep thoughts on issues, including Scripture, it will be a long road to gain wisdom. When we make mistakes, if we stop, accept the mistake, retry until we get it right, and then share that knowledge, we take a step towards wisdom. Most of us want the answer or "fix" right away so we can move on to the next pleasure or task ahead of us. Many of Jesus' parables were to instill wisdom in the listener. This is all predicated on a life of contemplation and study, something that seems to be getting more and more difficult as life is full of distractions and busyness.

Screwtape encourages his demons to keep humans caught up in the busyness of everyday life. This mirrors how modern society often values constant productivity and activity, leaving little time for spiritual reflection, yet ample time for immediate gratification. Just as alcohol provides immediate pleasure, modern distractions like social media offer instant satisfaction, potentially at the cost of long-term spiritual growth.

What are your distractors? Identify them and remove or lessen them in your days. If you are too busy and distracted, how will you ever hear the word of God?

During my summer holidays growing up in England and the United Kingdom, we would drive through the beautiful hills of Wales and marvel at what God has made. It gave me pause to contemplate the majesty of His creation and take a moment to thank Him for it. Compared to man-made technology, it pales in comparison. Smartphones, robots, and technology are complex and impressive, but I don't think people pick up their smartphones and marvel the same way they do when they look at God's creation. Look at what God has made; there's no comparison. Social media is designed to be addictive and to take you down pathways that leave you empty and unfulfilled. God is rarely in the mix on social media. Between marveling at creation and scrolling through social media, there is no comparison; one reveals God's glory, the other fades in an instant. There exists a stark contrast between humanity's fleeting experiences of awe, such as those found in nature, and the relentless trivialities that obscure divine truth.

One of the best ways to bring yourself into a closer relationship with Jesus Christ is to lessen the distractions and find time in the melee of life to connect with the Father, to be at one with God. You may need to get up before everyone else and pray while it is quiet and others are asleep, or go into nature, the beach, the mountains, or the wilderness, and talk to God. Unless we can find a way to add discipline to our lives and ignore the distractors, we won't be able to hear the voice of God. As Lewis vividly illustrates, the devil wanted to make the world so noisy that man would not hear the voice of God.

Fuddlement

A delightful old English word enters the conversation: "fuddled." It describes an intoxicating effect, being confused or stupefied. C. S. Lewis uses this term to capture the essence of the demonic mission: to "fuddle" or bewilder humanity. Distraction and fuddlement work hand in hand but are not the same. Distraction diverts our focus; fuddlement blurs it. In distraction, Satan pulls our attention away from what matters most. In fuddlement, he clouds our sight even while we're looking in the right direction. One misdirects; the other distorts. Both separate us from God.

The constant barrage of social media, misinformation, politics, health concerns, and carnal impulses are all tools Satan uses to create confusion and cloud our perspective. Yet we still have to navigate the ordinary routines of life. Even Jesus had to live in the mundane, He ate, rested, worked, and engaged with people about everyday matters. But even in the midst of life's ordinary rhythms, Jesus never allowed the mundane to blur His focus. His eyes remained fixed on the Father and on the things of eternal weight.

Most of us, in moments of prayer or reflection, have experienced distractions, a knock at the door, a ringing phone, or a sudden reminder of some task on our to-do list. Before we know it, the connection we were building with God slips quietly into the background. This is precisely the separation through fuddlement that the demonic seeks. They understand that the more we lean into God, the harder their work becomes, and the healthier we become.

Screwtape advises keeping humans "fuddled" and preoccupied with mundane concerns to prevent deep spiritual contemplation. Consider how easily we get caught up in daily noise: traffic, laundry, or deciding what to make for dinner. We often give these trivial matters more attention than they deserve, losing sight of what truly matters. When that happens, we unwittingly play into the Enemy's hands.

What does the demonic gain by intoxicating us with confusion? Let's first examine our relationships with others, then our relationship with God.

Most of us spend our days surrounded by people, but how deep are those connections? For many, they remain quite shallow. I once worked at a company where daily interactions revolved around surface-level small talk, everyone wearing the mask of "I'm fine, just doing my job." Beneath the surface, though, people were weary and hurting. When I started a small prayer group at the office, those same colleagues began to open up about their pain and struggles, seeking prayer for real issues. Fuddlement thrives in environments where relationships remain shallow, because it keeps our attention blurred and our compassion dulled. When we slow down long enough to truly see people, those barriers begin to fall away. We remember that relationships, loving our neighbor, carrying one another's burdens, are what really matter.

The effort required to maintain a façade creates barriers to genuine relationships. How can we love our neighbor if they never let us in? These struggles not only hinder healthy relationships but also open the door to unhealthy ones. Whether the issues are personal or rooted in family worries, it's difficult to focus on God while battling confusion. Yet praying for our friends and their families breaks the intoxicating grip of evil and clears our focus to draw closer to God.

When Screwtape uses the word "fuddled," it's a call to examine what might be clouding our judgment, what blurs rather than diverts. If you feel you don't have time to sit quietly or seek God, take a moment to consider what's fuddling you.

What patterns can you change to create space for clarity? Jesus showed us how to live within the ordinary without becoming lost in it, keeping His vision clear, His purpose steady, and His communion with the Father unbroken.

Jargon

Jargon are terms that are difficult for the common man to understand. To aid in that, we've provided a glossary of common words you will experience in your religious life on our website www.screwtapeletterspodcast.com.

Many of Jesus' teachings sought to explain complex ideas in simpler terms, offering illustrations that could be easily understood. His teaching method made truth accessible. As 1 John 3:2 reminds us, "Beloved, we are God's children now, and what we will be has not yet appeared; but we know that when he appears, we shall be like him, for we shall see him as he is." That verse reflects our desire to grow in understanding, to see Christ more clearly as we mature in faith and knowledge. Pursuing doctrine helps us move toward that clarity, as long as it draws us closer to Him and not away.

Theology is important. Really important! Clearly articulating truth claims, and biblical propositions is essential for following Jesus and navigating life. But the pursuit of doctrine can be a double-edged sword. While Scripture admonishes us to rightly divide the Word of truth and to teach sound doctrine, it also warns that knowledge can "puff up." A good thing, when taken too far or guided by pride, can easily become a problem. We must remember that we worship Jesus, not facts about Jesus. When theology becomes an idol, or when complex terms are preferred over simple ones, we see jargon doing its work. The demonic realm loves nothing more than to see language about God become an obstacle to knowing Him.

I vividly remember sitting in a packed church and listening to a passionate pastor unpack Scripture, referencing Greek and Hebrew translations. While his intent was to enrich our understanding, I noticed that some people seemed lost or disconnected, unable to follow the deeper discussion. The words we use matter. They shape our conversations, influence how people perceive us, and determine how well we connect. There's great beauty in studying Scripture deeply, but our learning should build bridges, not barriers.

Many believers, Catholic and Protestant alike, struggle with terms that can feel foreign or overly academic. Few Catholics, for example, could explain what *consubstantial* means in the Creed. Many non-denominational churchgoers don't understand the meaning of words like *transfiguration*, *supplication*, *eschatology*, or *gnosticism*. These words have deep theological roots, but without proper explanation, they can create distance instead of understanding.

This is where the demonic gains ground, when language meant to illuminate becomes a fog that alienates. Bible study thrives when people first feel invited, included, and inspired. If the words from the pulpit fail to connect, people will feel disengaged. And when that happens, the enemy celebrates, because confusion and pride have succeeded in separating people from the Word and from the One who gave it. Let doctrine deepen your love, not inflate your ego. Let your study of Scripture make you more approachable, not more detached. When theology leads us closer to Jesus, and brings others with us, it fulfills its true purpose.

Takeaway

The Enemy works through distraction, jargon, and fuddlement to keep our minds clouded and our hearts distant from God. He fills our days with noise and our faith with unnecessary complexity, until what should be simple begins to feel confusing or out of reach. The way back is through clarity and sincerity. Set aside the clutter, silence the noise, and speak with God plainly and honestly. You do not need perfect words or theological vocabulary to draw near to Him. Prayer is simply a conversation with your Creator, as you would speak with a good father or trusted friend. When you move past confusion and complication, you begin to experience the presence and peace that come only from walking closely with God.

A Closing Prayer

Lord, thank you for the gift of life! We ask for wisdom and guidance in making sure that we devote our time and energy towards things that really matter. Help us to grow in our knowledge of you while keeping our hearts in step along the way. Help us to identify and remove distractions so our days are not wasted. We pray against the Enemy who strives to keep us in a cloud of useless fuddlement. Lord, give us strong minds, quiet souls, and clear vision so we can walk in spirit and in truth and pursue the life you have for us. In Jesus' name, Amen!

Chapter 2
Imperfect Pews

As we sat down for our commentary on Letter 2, we couldn't help but reflect on our own experiences with church and faith. Like many believers, we have each walked through seasons of exploring different churches and wrestling with questions about denominational differences. Each tradition has its own beauty and challenges, and navigating those differences can be both enlightening and, at times, overwhelming.

We encourage you to reflect on your own experiences with church services. Consider moments when you may have felt uncomfortable or even judgmental toward those around you, feelings that may have ultimately worked to distance you or others from the church. Never forget that the church is a gathering of imperfect people, slowly and continually being transformed by the Lord. It's a journey we are all on together and none have arrived yet, yourself included.

Scripture

"And He put all things under His feet, and gave Him to be head over all things to the church, which is His body, the fullness of Him who fills all in all." - Ephesians 1:22-23

Resisting Spiritual Isolation

The demonic wants us to separate from the flock or from the church by making us uncomfortable. In Letter 2, we see the patient has become a newly converted Christian, facing the challenges of integrating into a community of believers, namely, the church. Screwtape, the senior demon, advises his nephew, Wormwood, on how to exploit this vulnerable period in the patient's spiritual journey.

The demonic strategy is often like apex predators in the wilderness. This helpful hunting technique help us visualize how this works. "It is an effective hunting technique. First, the target is separated from the herd; then, the hunters continually work until it is isolated and cannot count on the herd to protect it or warn it of danger. When the isolation is complete, the hunters put their strategy in place to destroy the animal. Their goal is only death and destruction for the animal, an important warning to all of us."

The church is so much more than a building, it's a sacred assembly and community of believers. For the new believer, church is a place where so many pivotal questions are asked and subjects explored: How did God create this world, and why exactly? Did I choose Him, or did He choose me? Is the Bible truly the breathed Word of God? How much of it is relevant, accurate, and divine? Will I hear God, see God, or experience God in church? Which church should I go to? Do I have to tithe? Should I be charitable? Can I just do church at home on video? So many questions. I have often asked people to and even outright told people to go to church. While no church is perfect, we cannot overlook the importance and benefits of being part of a community of faith centered around Jesus.

My experiences in various churches have been diverse and enlightening. Throughout my life, I've attended a wide range of religious gatherings, from Protestant and Catholic masses to

Evangelical services. Each denomination and congregation has its unique way of conducting worship, which can be both fascinating and, occasionally, jarring for newcomers.

While recalling aspects of my journey, I found myself transported back to my Catholic roots, remembering the familiar pews and the sense of community in the local churches in Coventry. At St. John Fisher, families had their usual places to sit each week; it was like we had season tickets. The looks of disdain when someone was sitting in the wrong place were palpable. Catholic Mass has all the traditions and dogma that, to someone who did not grow up in the Catholic church, would make them very uncomfortable. The sacrament of communion is excluded for those who are not Catholics; they will give you a blessing, but not the consecrated elements.

In Evangelical and Non-denominational churches, I've noticed a tendency towards more informal services, often with contemporary music and less structured liturgy. The atmosphere can vary greatly, from small, intimate gatherings to large, high-energy services with professional quality, produced worship music, and video production. More modern churches engage a variety of senses, from live, loud, charismatic, passionate worship music to deep-dive and damnation sermons, as they cover books of the Bible in depth.

The Bible instructs believers on how to live out their faith together and lays out a few essentials for what the church ought to do. Namely, meet together to break bread, pray, worship, and teach and preach the Word of God. But the Lord didn't go into great detail on exactly how we are to do those things. The only thing he really promised is that He will build His church and the Gates of Hell won't prevail against it. Fast forward 2000 years across nearly countless cultures around the globe, and you get a lot of different "flavors" of what church can look and feel like. And every stripe is made up of, and even led by, imperfect people. This is why we feel it is so important to build your life on a relationship with Jesus Christ and pursue being part of a local church with a heart and spirit that is humble, teachable, and discerning.

Resisting a Critical Spirit

One thing I have often struggled with as my walk with Christ has developed is learning how to strive for the best without taking on a spirit of criticism. Throughout my life, and especially the older I get, I've noticed my soul continually craves beauty. And I long for this especially when meeting together to worship God with His people. After all, where should beauty and excellence be on display if not in the church?! But if I'm being honest, my critical eye has struggled to withhold judgment when I see something in a church that, according to my "humble" standard, seems to… fall short. I often see churches struggling to create an inviting environment or find ways to communicate the Word of God in a way that is worthy of its glory. It's easy to get stuck in a rut with things like aesthetics and atmosphere. Interior design, stage design, music style and execution, visual aids, or lack thereof, and digital or print materials are all aspects of a church service that can either compel a heart to worship or distract from it.

I often feel like Wormwood's patient in his newfound church, gazing critically at the people and surroundings as if I'm superior to them in some way and asking myself, "THIS is church?!" In short, yes, it is. People from every tribe, tongue, demographic, socioeconomic class, educational background, and even political party coming together with one thing in common: faith in Jesus and a desire to worship Him. When I am reminded of this, I realize just how awful it is of me to take on a haughty eye or judgmental spirit. After all, the Lord saved me and accepted me to make me part of the body of Christ. And I realize Satan could not be more pleased than for me to distance myself from the church due to a smug and critical spirit towards the people that Jesus has determined to save and sanctify. A motley crew of which I am no doubt a ranking member.

As I continued to explore the letter, I was struck by the demons' attempts to foster a judgmental attitude in the patient. They wanted him to mock and criticize others, effectively thinking like a demon himself. I realized how this strategy could easily lead to discomfort and ultimately discourage people from returning to church.

It is easy to mock those who are too churchy, a little overzealous, smug, too hairy, too clean-cut, and so on. The people you are surrounded by at church are probably the top reason that people don't stick to a particular church. It is a shared experience, and when the worship and sermons are over, you spend time with these people. This is when the whispers amplify, where it is easy to find fault and lean into being judgmental.

The demonic want us to question whether these flawed individuals around us in the church could truly be the people of God. We are, by nature, the hunter, and the hunted, which has us put our guard up in situations that are new or otherwise uncomfortable for us. The demonic are working to plant seeds of doubt in our minds so we don't return to church. When every testimony on the stage is from someone who used to be violent, a criminal, an alcoholic, or a porn addict, and even the pastor has a chequered past, one may ask, "Where the heck am I?" That is one of the most beautiful parts of a church. It welcomes the imperfect, all of us sinners, and exists to help us turn our lives around. I could almost hear Screwtape's voice urging Wormwood to highlight every imperfection, every peculiarity that might make the patient uncomfortable or critical.

Seek To Understand Before Seeking to Be Understood

Whether you are a new believer or have been walking with Jesus for a long time, here's a practical approach to navigating a church with humility and discernment: Ask a lot of questions in good faith. For your own personal growth and journey, you should be asking questions about doctrine, the Bible, and this faith walk.

Many churchgoing Christians believe it is wrong to question their minister, Scripture, or church tenets. This plays right into the hands of the demonic. If you are not prepared to ask tough questions and discuss Scripture's meaning, you open yourself up to attack. In what ways is God's truth attacked by Satan in our day and age? The reason we titled this book *Confronting Evil in Our Time* was for that exact reason. How do Scripture and God's law from thousands of years ago affect us today? The 10 Commandments, for example, are as relevant today as they were thousands of years ago. Most Western societies' laws are predicated on them in large part.

If we don't continually ask questions for the sake of learning truth, we'll slowly become disarmed by passivity and ignorance. As believers, we should be well-versed in doctrine and able to defend truth in the variety of ways it is attacked today. This will make us more discerning of the teaching we hear and allow us to share and defend our faith to a world that dismisses the truth of God.

However, new believers should ask questions to gain knowledge, rather than to poke holes or impart their insight. There's a fine line between offering a fresh perspective and having a naive or uninformed opinion. As a pastor, I've spent countless hours lending an ear to new believers about perceived flaws in church methods, programming, and doctrine. My heart is to honor people as God's creation and help them grow in their knowledge and faith. More often than not, I found myself feeling like a pupil while the member was a teacher blessing me with their wisdom. The focus should be on seeking to understand rather than seeking to be understood. Great questions are welcome. Questioning aligns with Jesus' own teachings in seeking understanding.

Here's another great question to ask to make sure your heart is in the right place: "What can I do to help within my church?" First, spend time in your church home to get acquainted with everything it offers before you question things. Serve in your church. There is no better way to see the immense effort that goes into putting on a service and running church programming. Sometimes helping out in kids' ministry can teach you more about the heart of God than eight hours of deep Bible study. Fight the pull to be selfish and want things the way you like them. Take on the heart and mind of Christ in seeking knowledge and serving others.

Takeaway

We have a profound appreciation for the challenges new believers face when connecting with God and finding a church home. The journey can feel overwhelming amid the variety of worship styles, denominational differences, and imperfect people. Yet the church, at its best, is an assembly of God's people washed in the blood of Christ, led by the Holy Spirit, faithful to Scripture, and ready to "Put on the whole armor of God..."

I like to employ the 80/20 rule with any church. As long as I am comfortable with at least 80% of it, then I have a home. I don't mean 80% of the essentials like core doctrine or belief in Scripture. After all, Lewis declares, "The documents are complete and cannot be added to." I'm talking about 80% of the non-essentials: the building, parking, worship music, hymns, leadership, carpets, chairs, or people.

I'm willing to let go of the 20% of things in order to find a healthy church home. I don't want to be too picky. I am not going to let the demonic use silly reasons to pull me away from my church. It is too important.

A Closing Prayer

Lord, thank you for saving me! Thank you for taking my stubborn heart, blind eyes, and messy life and transforming it by the power of your Spirit and the work of Jesus on the cross. Thank you for your church and for helping me to find my place in what Jesus is building to advance against the gates of Hell. I pray for people in my life who can build me up and strengthen my walk with Jesus. And I ask that you would use me to do the same in the lives of others. In Jesus' name, Amen!

Chapter 3
Pitfalls of Spiritual Growth

Often in life, we encounter relationships, whether with family, friends, or coworkers, that, for no clear reason, seem marked by tension, conflict, or even outright strife. We may identify small issues, but upon reflection, they often appear too minor to explain the depth of the division. These relational difficulties frequently point to deeper emotional and spiritual dynamics at play. In particular, new believers may find that their relationships come under subtle but persistent spiritual attack, daily pinpricks meant to exploit character flaws and immaturity in faith.

These moments, while challenging, offer powerful opportunities to reflect, grow in wisdom, and mature spiritually. As with all matters of the heart and soul, the enemy seeks to sow discord, but through the power of Jesus Christ, we can begin to understand, heal, and strengthen our connections with others.

Scripture

"What causes quarrels and what causes fights among you? Is it not this, that your passions are at war within you?" - *James 4:1*

Relationships are Revealing

There is an interesting aspect of the demonic: collaboration. It's widely understood that demons work together with a sense of coordinated effort, operating with a hierarchical structure and maintaining a unified mission. Oftentimes, this is aimed at destroying the relationships that God designed for us to enjoy. We emerge from the womb, meet our parents, and are embraced with loving arms. But it doesn't take long to see the reality of the sin nature in ourselves and others. As we grow, we become self-determined, disobey our parents, experience conflict with peers and siblings, and in adulthood, we see the same with co-workers, spouses, and eventually children. Enjoying healthy relationships is not something that comes free or easy.

Since the beginning, in the garden and throughout the Bible, families have often clashed against each other: mothers against sons, fathers against sons, and brothers against brothers. Even the story of the prodigal son shows how a sibling relationship can be soured by jealousy and selfishness. The demonic no doubt love to see this, and beyond that, they seem to know how to pull the strings of flaws and sins to fan the flames of relational tension.

C. S. Lewis, in Letter 3, explores how the demonic Wormwood and Glubose work together to create division between the patient and his mother. Close family relationships create the perfect opportunity for us to see our imperfections and immaturities. It's only through the mirror of close human relationships that we can see the aspects of our personalities and character that need to be grown, matured, and given to the Lord. We can either face them, repent, and grow. Or harden our hearts in stubbornness and pride. And just like with Wormwood's patient, here we see the subtle sabotage of our relationships as a prime target of the demonic. We need to embrace the reality of our need to grow and lean on the Lord to guide the way.

Change in the New Believer

The Christian life is a transformation that involves both radical and gradual change. When a person comes to faith in Jesus, the Holy Spirit brings about an immediate and radical change. Scripture tells us that the heart is brought to life like a stone turning into flesh. Eternal destiny and identity are transformed from life apart from the Lord to enjoying eternity as a child of the King. We are spiritually brought from death to life, and the deepest part of the soul is impacted in a way that transforms every one of our desires.

But there's also an aspect of life in Christ that is very gradual. The Bible refers to this as sanctification, the slow process of bringing every aspect of our lives into conformity with what the Lord says we are and should be. These changes take time. It takes time to realize the foolish or selfish areas of our lives. And not only does it take time to see these things, but it takes time to change our actions and make those course corrections. In short, life with Jesus is a radical transformation that starts immediately in the heart, which then slowly starts to affect the things on the outside, like our actions and relationships.

Understanding sanctification is incredibly helpful, especially for new believers. It creates an environment where people feel free to cling to the powerful, radical work that God has done in their life while also being able to say honestly, "I'm still a work in progress!" This is absolutely crucial for healthy relationships. Having the freedom to be open and honest about our own shortcomings and blind spots allows us to address and resolve relational issues rather than allowing resentments to continually build.

New Christians who are on fire for the Lord are often taking in a firehose of new information, thoughts, emotions, prayers, and Scripture, trying to make sense of it all during this period of transformational change. It takes a while to become comfortable with the depth of faith and become wise about life. New Christians are vulnerable as they feel armed with righteousness and religious law, strutting around like a rookie police officer with new powers, looking to pin crimes on people breaking the same law they swore to uphold. This is the danger of immaturity mixed with spiritual zeal; it tends to spotlight others while avoiding the mirror.

Consider the ways in which we may have a double standard that applies to others but not ourselves, or how we expect grace and patience with our shortcomings but not with theirs. Allowing the mind of Christ to be present in the midst of a relationship means looking out for the well-being of others as if it were our own. The demonic will always exploit the flesh, which is naturally selfish and inwardly focused, but the mind of Christ causes us to look outward. This is a hallmark of emotional maturity, and it doesn't come easily. Age is automatic, but maturity takes work. And there are no shortcuts to being emotionally and spiritually mature.

A walk with the Trinity, God, Jesus, and the Holy Spirit, should lead us to deeper self-reflection and personal growth. It's not a license to highlight the flaws of others, especially the very people God has placed close to us. What then do we do when we have tension and disagreement in our relationships? Forgive, repent, and extend grace, remembering that we are all a work in progress.

Crossing the Wires

I'd like to introduce a concept that we see often in life. I call it crossing the wires. It's not necessarily committing an overt sin. It's simply overemphasizing or underemphasizing something in a way that causes our actions to be misguided. Satan seems keenly aware of this pitfall and exploits it every chance he gets. C. S. Lewis observes this throughout *The Screwtape Letters*. Let me explain.

I once pulled over to help a family whose car battery had died. I'd done this countless times before, pulled out my jumper cables, connected the batteries, and gave them a jumpstart. But this time, something went wrong. The wires started getting incredibly hot, and I saw smoke! I quickly realized my mistake: I'd mixed up the positive and negative terminals and accidentally crossed the wires. A simple, safe procedure I'd done a thousand times became dangerous in an instant, risking thousands of dollars in damage and potential bodily harm.

Our spiritual and relational lives work the same way. The right action at the wrong time, or the wrong emphasis in the right moment, can cause real damage. We might express anger when we should show mercy, stay silent when we should speak up, or focus on the spiritual when we need to address the practical. It's not always easy to know what's best in every moment, but what matters is remaining humble, reflective, and seeking wisdom daily.

In Letter 3, Screwtape shows exactly how this works. He advises Wormwood to keep the patient overly focused on his inner spiritual life, his prayers, his Bible reading, his conversion experience. All good things! But here's the trap: while the patient is consumed with his transformed heart, he's ignoring his transformed actions. He's so focused on what God is doing inside him that he neglects what God wants to do through him, especially toward his mother.

Could you imagine living with someone who's suddenly on fire for God, deeply invested in prayer and Scripture, but still leaves dishes in the sink and laundry on the floor? Maybe you don't have to imagine! The patient's mother doesn't need lectures about his spiritual transformation. She needs him to show up practically, with kindness, consideration, and basic helpfulness around the house. His focus isn't wrong; it's just misplaced. That's crossed wires. This is why spiritual maturity requires more than passion; it requires wisdom and awareness. As we grow in faith, we must learn to direct our transformed hearts toward transformed actions, especially in the relationships God has placed closest to us.

Praying on Point

One area that is particularly important to make sure our intentions and actions are properly directed is in the matter of prayer. New believers, although they mean well, sincerely so, without experience or guidance, even their prayers can become distorted. Instead of learning to love and understand the people around them, they pray for a version of that person that may not even exist.

Take the example of a young believer praying fervently for a family member or a neighbor. "Lord, please save them. Change their heart. Make them soft and moldable. Bring them to Your light." The impulse to intercede is good, but sometimes it's a way of venting frustration disguised as spirituality. In praying for someone's "soul," they bypass the opportunity to engage with that person's actual needs and circumstances. They may not notice that the person is already saved. Or they may ignore that the real issue isn't the other person's lack of faith, it's their own lack of humility, patience, or practical love.

Lewis captured this brilliantly in this letter, where Screwtape instructs Wormwood to get the patient to pray for his mother's soul, anything to keep him from praying for her health, her habits, her practical burdens, or their relationship. In other words: keep the prayer lofty and disconnected. Get him praying for her soul while ignoring her humanity. And that's how well-meaning Christians can end up praying for fictional versions of people, constructed from frustrations, assumptions, and immaturity. These prayers may sound spiritual, but they bypass the heart of the gospel: seeing people as God sees them, in truth and love.

So, what is the solution? Prayer, yes, but not prayer that becomes a blindfold. Rather, prayer that invites God to reveal the full picture. Prayer that starts with, "Lord, search me." Prayer that includes, "Help me to see this person rightly. Help me love them as they are, not as I imagine them to be."

The power of prayer goes beyond what we think is possible. It is a divine connection, unpolluted by demonic interference, a line between Creator and child that cannot be tapped or tampered with. But the clarity of that connection depends, in part, on whether we are praying from a place of humility or self-righteousness.

Yes, pray for healing. Yes, pray for salvation. But also pray for wisdom. Pray for understanding. Pray for awareness. Some of the most important prayers we can offer are not "Change them," but "Change me."

As new believers grow in their faith, they must learn to pray not just with fire, but with light. Passion without perspective leads to praying for illusions. And when we pray for someone, we don't even truly know, someone we've reduced to a list of grievances or hopes, we end up missing both the person and the power of prayer.

Takeaway

God radically transforms our hearts the moment we come to faith, but shaping our actions and relationships takes time. The demonic exploit this gap, using our immaturity and misplaced priorities to damage the very relationships God gave us to enjoy. When we "cross the wires," focusing on the spiritual while neglecting the practical, or praying for someone's soul while ignoring their actual needs, we play right into the enemy's hands. The solution isn't perfection, but humility. Before reacting impulsively, pray and reflect. Forgive quickly, extend the grace you'd hope to receive, and remember that we are all works in progress. Let your transformed heart lead to transformed actions, especially toward those closest to you.

A Closing Prayer

Lord, thank you for a radical change in my heart! I pray that as I grow in my walk of faith, you will show me my blind spots, grow me in my maturity, and help me view others the way you view them. May the work you do in me bring about healthy relationships as you designed. Give me wisdom to know when my flesh or the enemy is subtly pulling me to be unfair or misguided. Help me to be humble every day to become everything you have made me to be. In Jesus' name, Amen!

Chapter 4
The Enduring Power of Prayer

In our relationship with God, there is almost nothing that the demonic wants more than to stop us from praying and connecting with our heavenly Father. God designed prayer to be our access to his presence for continual dialogue. It's our way of petitioning for our needs and desires, expressing gratitude and praise, and laying our hearts bare before Him, and seeking His heart and mind in all things.

Prayer truly is the daily lifeline for God's people to walk in ongoing fellowship and obedience. And like the war tactic of strategically attacking the enemy's lines of communication, the demonic is literally hellbent on stopping and distorting prayer in any way they can. Screwtape makes sure Wormwood is well aware of this point.

Scripture

"Be anxious for nothing, but in all things by prayer and supplication, with thanksgiving, let your requests be made known to God; and the peace of God, which surpasses all understanding, will guard your hearts and minds through Christ Jesus." - Philippians 4:6-7

What is Prayer, and Why is it Important?

Prayer is a part of a genuine relationship with God. It's not merely a performative or emotional exercise. And as such, our prayers should be dynamic and real. They should be a mix of spontaneous and planned, private and public, impromptu and scripted, free-flowing verbal expression to the Lord, and also liturgical traditions like "The Lord's Prayer." When we practice prayer authentically and pursue it as a spiritual discipline, we grow our faith and relationship with God.

Paul says in 1 Thessalonians 5:17 that we should "Rejoice always, pray without ceasing, give thanks in all circumstances." The idea of constantly practicing thankfulness and petitioning in your life is wonderful. We may not be able to pray every moment of every day, but our hearts can be continually seeking the Lord in all things and at all times. Start each day with a prayer for guidance, posture your heart to worship, take on an attitude of thankfulness for health and blessing, petition for abundance in provision for your family, and intercede with prayers of healing for others. Pray at home, in the shower, on your way to work, before a job interview, at meals, when you get home safely, and before you go to sleep. Prayer is something that should be an active, ongoing activity and way of life for the believer.

It's also important to know that prayer is not a one-way conversation; rather, it's a means by which the Lord speaks to and reveals things to us as we seek Him. And oftentimes with life-changing results. This means that prayer can be conversational. There are some that believe prayer is ONLY making a request made known to God. They'll often cite the fact that the meaning of the word prayer is "to ask." And while it's true the word does mean to ask, I'm not sure if we can stress enough that prayer is so much more than asking God for things! It's a continual conversation with a Heavenly Father who knows, loves, and cares for you. And unlike conversations with humans, sometimes prayer can even be a pouring out of your heart when you don't know what to say. Scripture tells us that the Spirit of God will pray when we can't find the words to speak, how great is that!? Prayer can even be just laying your troubles at the Lord's feet without an idea of what to say or what comes next.

There are aspects of prayer that people completely overlook and neglect. It's almost like the most powerful weapon in the battle of life that we so often forget to pick up. I challenge you to pray every day and become a seven-day Christian and not just a Sunday and Holy Days Christian; you WILL see remarkable things happen.

Authentic Prayer

Satan is well aware of the importance of prayer in the life of the believer. We see this as Screwtape advises Wormwood to pull the patient away from a pure and proper form of prayer. He highlights a number of ways that the patient can be distracted and effectively have his prayers rendered innocuous. Let's unpack some of these principles.

It's a powerful thing, having the God of heaven hear and answer our prayers. So, when talking about prayer, we need to focus on exactly where that power comes from. It's amazing to me how many people, myself included at times, if I'm being honest, feel that during prayer, I need to be conjuring up some sort of emotional and compelling moment. If you've ever had somebody pray for you in a powerful and dynamic way, it can feel inspiring and exciting. But that feeling does not always accompany prayer. We should be emotionally and intellectually engaged, but that doesn't mean we'll always "feel the power" in the moment. And it certainly doesn't mean that the prayer will be answered based on how well I prayed, or how I felt when I prayed.

Prayer is often surprisingly commonplace and ordinary. Which is what makes it one of the simplest forms of faith. You are speaking to a God that you cannot see and believe that he exists, hears you, and will do something about your request. If God didn't exist, you'd really look a fool talking to the air! So, it's the measure of the faith that empowers prayer, not the delivery or the excitement or the eloquence of what's said. This seems like such a simple fact, but I feel like it's one we often overlook. Almost to the point where we feel the need to manufacture feelings or responses.

In addition, our feelings become stumbling blocks to a meaningful prayer life; we also need to guard ourselves against thinking that other external things have power or influence in prayer. This happens when we fall victim to routine, regimen, or worse, religion. It can be easy to diminish God and reduce him to a building, even an ancient or new church or cathedral. God is omnipresent, meaning He is everywhere. One can pray sincerely with items like a crucifix or a rosary, but make sure you are not praying to the crucifix or rosary. It may sound simple, but it's amazing how our focus can gradually shift without even realizing it.

Yoga, Meditation, or "Being Spiritual"

When people say, "I'm spiritual," it echoes of the agnostic. It has no real definition other than "of the spirit." It's like wanting to connect to spiritual things without acknowledging the Holy Spirit (of the Trinity) or even discerning between the devil and the Lord. It waxes of drifting through life with ties to whatever whim excites, attracts, or entertains. It says, "I am not connected to any particular religion; I'm a free spirit." Who do "spiritual" people pray to? Often an undefined god, themselves, or possibly something worse!

Modern trends, particularly among younger generations, prioritize "authenticity" in spiritual practices. They lean into "keeping it real" when, of course, it becomes a mere tendency to cast away anything that may be perceived as conventional while embracing almost anything as long as it feels innovative. This often results in people creating a version of God who accepts and encourages every flaw they may have. This approach often leads to creating a customized spiritual experience that lacks theological depth and truth. Be careful what spirits you invite into your prayer life. We feel it's important to emphasize that prayer should be about connecting with God as He truly is, rather than creating a personalized version of a generic divinity that suits individual preferences. You don't make Him, He made you.

Yoga and meditation, as commonly practiced today, are forms of spirituality that focus on the self and opening oneself to undefined spiritual forces. If you believe you are a god, these practices align with that worldview. But for those seeking a relationship with Jesus Christ, there is a critical distinction to understand. Scripture does speak of meditation, but biblical meditation means contemplating the Word of God and communing with Him through prayer. It is focused, directed, and grounded in truth. Modern meditation, however, teaches something entirely different: emptying the mind, pursuing the self, and opening your body and spirit to whatever may enter.

While prayer is communing with the God of heaven through Jesus Christ, secular meditation is like opening all the doors to your house and inviting anything or anyone to come in. This undefined spirituality may seem harmless, but it opens doorways to the demonic and leads the spiritually curious down a path toward the occult, away from the one true God.

Common Pitfalls in Prayer

As we've walked with the Lord and led others in prayer, we've noticed some common patterns that tend to undermine our connection with God. Here are a few pitfalls to watch out for in your own prayer life:

- Turning your gaze on yourself
- Preventing genuine self-reflection
- Maintaining superficial spiritual practices
- Viewing God as we believe He is or should be
- Avoiding silence and solitude with the Lord
- Making yourself the god you worship
- Preventing you from praying altogether
- Making prayer a transactional moment

These are the kinds of subtle traps that can creep into anyone's spiritual life. If you recognize any of these patterns, you've identified where the enemy may be working.

Healing Prayer

While Lewis in Letter 4 doesn't talk about specific types of prayer or things to pray for, we wanted to take the opportunity to use this chapter on prayer to discuss something we both feel strongly about: praying in faith for healing.

Anyone who has attended an evangelical church service has heard the call for healing and even sometimes witnessed a healing on stage. Although skepticism abounds about those moments, be open to them. I have witnessed healing through prayer, though it's not magic nor instantaneous.

I have been part of and led prayer groups, in the name of Jesus, for the sick and the empirical medical community has made comments like, "The healing is nothing short of miraculous," "This doesn't happen," "They shouldn't be alive," or "We gave them no more than a few days, pulled them off life support, and now they are sitting up eating ice cream." One doctor even got on the phone with us and said, "Whatever you did, please do more of it!" As much as we value and honor the medical community, we look to Jesus as God, not the doctors. And we believe that when we pray in faith, He can and will do the miraculous! Mark 16:17-18 says, "And these signs will follow those who believe: In my name… they will lay hands on the sick, and they will recover."

A Healing of "Faith"

When my son suffered severe head trauma with a double brain bleed at, of all places, Bible camp, we received the phone call that he was in the ICU in Flagstaff, AZ, and that we should make the two-hour trip immediately. The head trauma doctor told us that these situations don't generally end well, that our son would probably not be the same going forward, and that we should be prepared for that eventuality if he makes it through the next 48 hours. What the medical community knows about head trauma is still a work in progress. The outcome is a matter of luck and prayer.

My immediate reaction was to pray. My wife and I held our son's hand and prayed over him constantly. For the next 11 days, I prayed continually, and through text threads with everyone who loved him, wanting updates, I prepared prayers for them to gather and pray together. We had several churches praying for my son, as well as family and friends from all around the world.

Fourteen days later, my son had passed all of the cognitive tests and, against the advice of his doctor, returned to school in person. He had made a "remarkable recovery."

Some doubters asked if we "maybe overreacted with his diagnosis," or "maybe it wasn't as bad as first thought." Interestingly, more effort is used to deny and disprove the power of healing prayer than to accept it. Although it is understandable that if they, too, had prayed and not seen a positive result, then why us and not them?

My son's lasting symptom is a lack of a sense of smell, as his olfactory nerves were damaged when his brain was raked across his skull base. It's a small reminder that he was healed, is human, and is not invincible like God. I think it has also strengthened his walk of faith.

Takeaway

Finding a place for solitude, not isolation, is tremendously important for prayer. Go out into nature, find a quiet place at home, enjoy a long walk, or find an empty church where you can hear your heartbeat and the echoes of God in the structure. Don't reduce prayer to a purely emotional or feeling-based activity. Instead, effective prayer involves discipline, structure, and a willingness to engage with God beyond our immediate emotional state. Still, maintain an open, vulnerable heart while seeking to understand God as He truly is, not as we wish Him to be. The effect and joy of full intimacy with God is incalculable. We'll end this chapter with the words of Jesus in John 16:23-24, "Most assuredly, I say to you, whatever you ask the Father in My name He will give you. Until now you have asked nothing in My name. Ask, and you will receive, that your joy may be full."

A Closing Prayer

Dear Lord, thank you for giving me access to your throne. Thank you for sharing your heart and mind and will. Thank you for hearing the requests of your people and having a heart to always provide what I need. Help me to always approach you and see you as you are, not as how I think you should be. Help me to always be open and honest and lay my heart before you. Holy Spirit, thank you for praying when I don't know exactly what to say. And please give me ears to hear and discernment to know when you are speaking. In Jesus name, Amen.

Chapter 5
Confronting Evil in Our Time

Letter 5 explores how Christians make moral choices and respond to human suffering amid war's grim realities and life's deepest trials, from geopolitical conflicts to personal crises. How does God engage with His people through these moments of profound struggle? It's an age-old question.

God's people have faced wars and endured great suffering throughout the Bible and human history. This doesn't necessarily mean God endorses war or hardship, as they are tragic outcomes of human brokenness and free will. But the vital question for Christians is how we respond to these times of intense difficulty and evil. Allowing suffering to strengthen our faith as we stand up for what God says is right is what will turn horrific atrocities into stories of redemption.

Scripture

"Therefore take up the whole armor of God, that you may be able to withstand in the evil day, and having done all, to stand firm." – Ephesians 6:13

The Ugliness and Reality of War

The Screwtape Letters were written during the start of World War II, a war that was never supposed to happen; the end of World War I was to be the "war to end all wars." Yet here we were, 20 years later, back at it in Europe. This time, though, the war wasn't restricted to trenches on the borders of France; it was global.

The end of World War I in 1918 was heralded with hopes for lasting peace and international cooperation. The Treaty of Versailles, signed in 1919, imposed harsh penalties on Germany, including territorial losses, military restrictions, and reparations payments. This agreement aimed to prevent future German aggression. Simultaneously, the League of Nations was established as an international organization to maintain world peace through collective security and disarmament. Founded on principles of diplomacy and arbitration, the League sought to prevent future conflicts. However, despite these efforts, human mechanisms ultimately failed to prevent the rise of Nazi Germany and the outbreak of World War II, demonstrating the complex challenges of maintaining global peace.

The Axis powers, formed during World War II, primarily consisted of Nazi Germany, Fascist Italy, and Imperial Japan. (Not to be confused with the "Axis of Evil" which was a term coined by President George W. Bush in 2002, referring to Iraq, Iran, and North Korea, which was used in the context of the post-9/11 War on Terror.) These nations were united in their aggressive expansionist policies and totalitarian ideologies. Nazi Germany, led by Adolf Hitler, was responsible for the Holocaust, systematically murdering millions of Jews, and other minority groups. They also initiated the war in Europe through invasions of neighboring countries. Imperial Japan, under Emperor Hirohito, committed numerous atrocities in Asia, including the Rape of Nanking and the brutal treatment of prisoners of war.

Fascist Italy, led by Benito Mussolini, engaged in colonial conquests in Africa and supported Nazi Germany's actions. The Axis powers were collectively accused of war crimes, crimes against humanity, and attempts to establish a new world order based on racial supremacy and authoritarian rule. The world, as it had many times before, had no choice but to interact with the ugly reality of evil and suffering.

Why does a good God allow such evil? The demonic relish mankind's destruction and evil's spread in war, yet it's not a clear win for them, as trials and suffering often lead men to cry out to God. Adversity draws out the best and the worst of humanity. War is a challenge that deeply impacts faith, family, and country. You know the perils of inaction when evil is at your door, but you also know the conflict in your heart when you are called to step up to kill those who mean to kill you, your family, your friends, and countrymen.

War's devastation brings about human suffering, an unfortunate reality not just of war but of life itself. God, knowing this, designed life to walk with His people through pain, most powerfully shown through Christ's journey. Jesus endured betrayal, abandonment, torture, mockery, and a brutal death on the cross, revealing a God who intimately understands suffering. From Job's trials to Christ's sacrifice, Scripture shows God meeting us in our darkest moments, offering grace to endure, and often restoring and redeeming the pain. History and faith reveal that in suffering, while some may turn from God, many find Him, drawing closer in the midst of their trials.

An Error of Extremes

In times of war and suffering, Christians often fall into one of two extremes: ignoring evil entirely or becoming consumed by fighting it. Both miss the mark. The first extreme effectively pretends the world's brokenness can't or shouldn't be addressed, clinging to a naive optimism that avoids the reality of sin and its consequences. This can lead to passivity, where believers fail to confront evil or engage with the world's pain. The second extreme fixates on human mechanisms as the solution to right all wrongs. It risks turning righteousness into a crusade driven by national pride or human strength. In *The Screwtape Letters*, the demonic strategy is to push believers into either becoming what Screwtape calls an "extreme patriot" or an "ardent pacifist." Either extreme works for the demonic so long as the Christian loses sight of God's kingdom and their calling.

The pacifist error is an interesting one. It's often cloaked in spiritual language that sounds biblical. Many believers are tempted toward complete disengagement from conflict and cultural involvement in the name of peace. It seems noble on the surface. After all, didn't Jesus say, "blessed are the peacemakers"? Doesn't Scripture say, "Thou shalt not kill"?

But here's where things go off track. The 10 Commandments, as found in Exodus 20 and Deuteronomy 5, are often misunderstood, as many translations say, "Thou shalt not kill." However, the idea is more accurately explained when the translation from the Hebrew is "You shall not murder" (Lo Tirtzach). This distinction is critical. Scripture forbids unjust, premeditated killing, not all taking of life under any circumstances. The Bible also acknowledges and regulates things like self-defense, capital punishment, and warfare. In fact, God institutes the death penalty for certain crimes as early as Genesis 9, declaring that human life is sacred and must be protected by just consequences.

God has not called His people to passive withdrawal. We were made to take ground from the demonic. To shape culture, lead with righteousness, and stand in the gap where injustice spreads. In a world where evil thrives when unopposed, absence is not neutrality; it's complicity. The devil rejoices when God's people abdicate their call to be salt and light and hands and feet, because wherever there's a void, the powers of darkness are happy to fill it.

When it comes to knowing when it's proper and appropriate to engage in warfare, there's a helpful principle known as the "Just War Theory," which has evolved over time. Though the Bible doesn't spell out a "just war checklist," Christian thinkers across the centuries, from Augustine to Aquinas, have drawn on Scripture to frame a theology of warfare. Just War Theory proposes that war can be morally permissible under certain conditions:

- Just Cause - War must confront a grave evil or threat
- Legitimate Authority – War must be declared by a duly constituted body
- Right Intention - Its aim must be peace, not conquest or revenge
- The use of force must be proportionate and discriminate, minimizing harm to civilians

These principles don't glorify war. They constrain it. They reflect the painful reality that, while we await the full arrival of God's kingdom, we sometimes must take up arms against injustice to preserve life and defend the innocent.

So why does the enemy push so hard for pacifism? Because the world is shaped by those who act. If the people of God cower in the name of peace, who will push back against the chaos? The devil doesn't need every believer to be violent; he just needs them to be absent. Because when the righteous step back, evil rushes in unchecked. Satan's lies, saying that holiness means staying out of the fight. In reality, holiness means knowing which fights matter, why they matter, and how to engage in them for the glory of God.

But on the other extreme, that of the extreme patriot, carries a different seduction. This view clings to the belief that we can usher in the Kingdom of God through the institutions of man. It takes the mandate to build, rule, and influence and stretches it into a belief that national systems and political ideologies can fix the world's problems if only the "right people" are in charge.

It's admirable in its optimism. The desire to stand for righteousness, protect the innocent, and reform broken systems is noble. But the danger lies in mistaking the tools of man for the power of God. As much as we are called to bring salt and light into our nations, we cannot confuse civic righteousness with spiritual rebirth. God alone changes hearts. No law, bill, politician, or party can regulate righteousness.

Sometimes the truth lives in tension. Just as we wrestle with divine sovereignty and human free will, we also must hold a dual reality, we are citizens of heaven and citizens of earth. We're called to shape the world, but we cannot save it. We should fight for justice and truth, but we must never mistake ourselves for the Savior.

Scripture reminds us that God originally didn't want Israel to have a human king. He desired to rule them directly. But the people insisted and wanted to be like other nations. That same impulse to trust in human authority to do what only God can, still tempts us today. We long for a leader who can make everything right. But no elected official, no matter how wise or principled, will usher in lasting peace. Even Satan masquerades as an angel of light, and Scripture seems to warn that even the Antichrist will rise under the banner of global peace.

We must be on guard. Christian nationalism, blind party allegiance, or the belief that our country is God's final plan for redemption are dangerous distortions. God created the nations, yes.

And Jesus died for the nations. We should seek the good of our cities and nations and do all we can to advance righteousness. But we cannot place our ultimate hope in the systems of man to achieve this. Only Christ can truly save us, and the devil would love nothing more than for Christians to forget this.

Stepping Up or Standing Down

Evil does not stop itself, it is not passive, it doesn't take days off, wait for permission, or go away on its own. It advances constantly, persistently, aggressively, and wherever it is not resisted. It fills vacuums and multiplies when no one says "No."

Diplomacy doesn't stop evil. That's been the false hope of nations and treaties for centuries. But evil doesn't respect lines on a map. It doesn't care about signatures or promises. Evil must be named, opposed, and stopped. And that responsibility falls squarely on the shoulders of God's people.

The book of Revelation rebukes the church in Thyatira not for what they did, but for what they allowed. They tolerated that woman Jezebel. They made peace with evil. They put up with it. And in every generation, the demonic counts on Christians doing the same. Not openly endorsing wickedness but just tolerating it. Standing back and staying quiet.

This is where the people of God must rise. Not in outrage or self-righteousness, but in steady, Spirit-led conviction. Whether you're confronting the evil of a tyrant, the destruction of unborn life, or the quiet cruelty in your own neighborhood, every believer has a role. Attend a Walk for Life rally or volunteer at a pregnancy center. Run for your school board or show up to meetings and speak up against ideologies that undermine parental authority and biblical truth.

Stand up for the reality of two genders, especially when children are being targeted with confusion. Support leaders and organizations that defend traditional marriage and the family. The public square belongs to Christians too; don't cede it to those who would use it to advance godlessness. You may not be on a battlefield, but you are in a war. And every inch of ground evil gains is ground someone gave up.

In Nazi Germany, Dietrich Bonhoeffer understood this. He watched as a so-called Christian nation compromised itself into collapse. He rejected the state church and helped form the remnant Confessing Church that held fast to the gospel. Eventually, he participated in a plot to assassinate Hitler over deep anguish about what was happening to his country and to the Jews. It cost him his life.

Bonhoeffer wasn't a radical. He was a pastor. A man of prayer. A man of peace. But his peace was not the peace of tolerance. It was the peace that comes when evil is confronted and righteousness is pursued. He believed, as Romans 13 suggests, that we submit to authority only in so much as it does not cause us to disobey God.

Scripture is full of examples like this. Shadrach, Meshach, and Abednego refused to bow even when the law demanded it. Peter stood before the courts and said, "We must obey God rather than men." These weren't men looking for a fight. They were men who knew where their ultimate allegiance lay.

The world doesn't drift toward righteousness. Left alone, everything collapses. Nations decay. Justice fades. Morality erodes. And the demonic is always ready to fill the gaps. Hell doesn't need a violent revolution to win. It just needs a distracted, passive, silent church.

That's the danger. Christians convince themselves that standing up isn't their job. They stay quiet, keep their heads down, and defer to someone else. And the devil is content to let them sulk in their suffering, as long as they stay on the sidelines. But the kind of Christian the enemy truly fears is the one who knows God's Word, walks in the Spirit, and stands without flinching when evil begins to rise.

Now let's be honest. We've spent this chapter warning against the extremes of the ardent pacifist and the extreme patriot. But if we're forced to choose between erring on the side of passivity or erring on the side of action, we'll choose action every time. Standing in the middle doesn't make you righteous. It often just makes you irrelevant. If people want to accuse us of being too engaged, too passionate, or too willing to fight the culture war, so be it. This is the cost of confronting evil. We answer to the Lord, not to men. And right now, in this moment of history, Christians need to be wise as serpents, gentle as doves, and more active than hell!

Takeaway

We live in a sin-cursed world with a natural pull toward destruction where evil flourishes unless it's actively resisted. In the face of war, pain, and injustice, we are tempted toward many errors: to withdraw into pacifism, to overextend into worldly activism, or to simply sulk in our suffering. But the call of God is higher. In the midst of suffering, there is redemption. In the face of evil, there is purpose. We are not called to cower or to conquer in our own strength, but to stand in His power and strength. Avoid the extremes. Reject the demonic distortions. And rise as the people of God, who know both how to suffer well, how to stand strong, and where necessary, confront evil.

A Closing Prayer

Lord, we thank You for the work of Jesus on the cross. We thank You that He is a God who understands pain and suffering in a sin-cursed world. And thank You that through His suffering, we have victory in all things. I pray that You would help me to know where and how I can stand up against evil, be an advocate for justice and righteousness, and live according to the Kingdom of God in the world today. In Jesus name, Amen.

Chapter 6
The Battlefield of Fear

On fear's battlefield, we see one of the greatest tactics of Satan in a variety of ways. Fear can be intense and consuming. Exploiting fear is an ancient tactic that takes countless forms, from the terror of war to the quiet anxiety about tomorrow. Its purpose remains unchanged, to separate us from God. Being consumed by fear and having trust in the Lord are different realities and are contradictory emotions; one draws us toward heaven while the other pulls us toward hell.

Letter 6 unveils the depth and complexity of this spiritual struggle, showing how fear operates not only in times of crisis but in the ordinary moments of everyday life. Whether it manifests as dread about the future, paralyzing anxiety, or obsessive fixation on "what ifs," fear transforms the human heart and mind into a battlefield. Let's examine how demons exploit our fears, how irrational anxiety derails clear thinking, and how Christians can cultivate the courage to face fear armed with God's truth.

Scripture

"Have I not commanded you? Be strong and courageous. Do not be frightened, and do not be dismayed, for the Lord your God is with you wherever you go." - Joshua 1:9

Choosing Fear or Courage

Fear is a powerful force. It grips the heart, clouds the mind, and whispers lies about the future. The demonic know this well. Screwtape instructs Wormwood to make the patient experience "maximum uncertainty" about what lies ahead. This is the battlefield fear creates a place where our minds spin with endless possibilities of threats and dangers. Fear also doesn't need facts. It can thrive on imagination, on "what ifs," as it exploits the darkness of the unknown.

Courage is not the absence of fear, but rather "acting rightly in the midst of fear." It's the spiritual discipline of identifying the cross in front of you today, picking it up, and carrying it. Demonic forces try to prevent people from facing their "appointed cross" (real current challenges) by overwhelming them with crippling anxiety. And responding to fear with anxiety can become a habit. But courage can also become a habit. Courage is like a muscle. The more we exercise it, the stronger it becomes. Every time you choose to act rightly despite your fear, you build resilience. You train yourself to trust God's presence more than your circumstances. You learn that even when your hands shake and your heart pounds, you can still move forward in obedience.

This is where the choice comes in. Fear will present itself; that's inevitable. But how we respond is entirely up to us. Will we let fear paralyze us, or will we let it drive us toward God? Will we spiral into anxiety over threats, or will we take the next right step in faith?

The demonic want to keep us frozen, obsessing over threats that may never materialize. They flood our minds with fears about things far removed from the actual work God has given us today. Why? Because when we face real challenges with courage, we grow. Our faith strengthens. Our character deepens. And the enemy loses ground. But when we waste our energy dwelling on fear, we squander the strength God intended to fight battles that actually matter.

Faith puts our trust in God as we walk through difficulty, not around it. David understood this when he wrote in Psalm 23:4, "Yea, though I walk through the valley of the shadow of death, I will fear no evil; For You are with me." Notice he didn't say God would remove the valley. He said God would be with him in it. And that presence, that divine companionship, was enough to overcome fear.

So, the question becomes, what is your appointed cross today? Not the thousand disasters your mind wants to chase. Not the fears about next month or next year. What is the real challenge God has placed before you right now? That is where your courage is needed. That is where your faith will be tested and strengthened. And that is where God promises to meet you.

Irrational Fear in Our Time

We've all heard Franklin D. Roosevelt's famous declaration, "The only thing we have to fear is fear itself." Lewis echoed this wisdom so precisely that you'd wonder if he was listening when Roosevelt delivered these words in his 1933 inaugural address. Screwtape observes that "fear becomes easier to master when the patient's mind is diverted from the thing feared to the fear itself." This insight reveals a profound truth, we often experience fear not for tangible threats requiring immediate attention, but for a thousand imagined dangers that may never materialize.

Today, most of us live safer lives than any generation before us. Few face the immediate threat of war or violent crime. Yet we've become masters at manufacturing new anxieties. News outlets, as an example, desperate for engagement, know that tragedy sells. "If it bleeds, it leads," as the industry saying goes. We're drawn to horrifying headlines like moths to flame, and these stories plant seeds of fear even when the events are continents away from our daily lives. Consider how this works, a crocodile attack in Northern Australia makes people in Kansas afraid to swim in their local lake. A subway killing in New York causes someone in rural Montana to fear public transportation they'll never use. A tragic car accident becomes the catalyst for countless parents to deliver tearful lectures about driving safety to teenagers. These concerns aren't entirely without merit, but they're amplified far beyond reason by minds already primed for fear.

Why do we so readily consume irrational fears? Here's an irony worth pondering, many people reject the Bible because its stories seem unreasonable or hard to believe. Yet these same people eagerly consume a daily diet of sensationalized news, building a fortress of fear from events that will likely never touch their lives. They dismiss ancient wisdom as fantasy while constructing very real anxiety from modern fiction. Fear can become a prison of the mind, preventing us from seeing the blessings right in front of us. But we have powerful antidotes, worship and gratitude create an atmosphere of peace where fear cannot thrive. When we truly embrace our relationship with Christ, we discover a peace that no earthly circumstance can provide or destroy.

Yes, there are genuine threats in this world worthy of prudent caution. For our spiritual growth, we need the virtues of wisdom and discernment to recognize real dangers while refusing to be paralyzed by imaginary ones. The key is developing a balanced perspective on fear and courage, learning to distinguish between legitimate concerns that require action and phantom anxieties that only steal our joy.

True courage isn't the absence of fear; it's the ability to discern between real and imaginary threats and to act decisively when action is needed. This aligns perfectly with the Lord's most frequent command in the Bible, "Don't be afraid." Do you see what God is telling us? He knows our tendency toward fear and provides daily reminders that we need not be controlled by it.

The challenge before us is clear, recognize when our fears are irrational phantoms and learn to confront them with truth rather than allowing them to become our masters. Only then can we live in the freedom and peace God intends for His children.

Breaking the Cycle of Fear

Fear operates in cycles. It's not just a single emotion that comes and goes; it's a loop that reinforces itself over time. Think of it like a pathway through the woods. The first time you walk it, the ground is rough and uncertain. But the more you take that route, the more worn in it becomes. Eventually, it's the easiest path to follow, even if it's leading you somewhere you don't want to go. That's how fear works in our minds. Each time we respond to fear with passivity, avoidance, or panic, we deepen the rut. We train ourselves to be fearful. And the demonic are more than happy to keep us walking that same beaten path.

The good news is that courage works the same way. As we mentioned earlier, fearfulness and courage both function like muscles; the more we use them, the stronger they become. The key is making sure we're training the right one. Every time you choose courage in the face of fear, you're carving out a new pathway. You're building a new habit. And over time, that becomes your default response. By God's grace, we can break the cycle of fear and even reverse it.

To break the cycle, it helps to recognize how we're hardwired to respond to danger. It's generally understood that we naturally default to one of four instinctual reactions: freeze, flee, fight, or fawn.

These responses aren't sinful in themselves; they're embedded deeply within us as survival mechanisms. But left unchecked, they become our automatic patterns, and the demonic exploit them. Freeze becomes paralysis. Flee becomes cowardly avoidance of responsibility. Fight becomes misplaced aggression. Fawn becomes appeasement and passivity dressed as peacekeeping. The goal of spiritual maturity is not to eliminate these instincts, but to subject them to wisdom, faith, and discernment. We learn to evaluate our gut reactions and align them with God's will, choosing courage over reflex.

The vital discipline is feeding your mind with noble truth. If you fill your mind with God's wisdom in advance, truth will be there when fear strikes. This is why Scripture commands us to "guard your heart and mind in Christ Jesus" - Philippians 4:7. It's where we see the battles of spiritual warfare. The ancients, warriors, and prophets alike trained their minds as diligently as they trained their bodies. Truth is ultimately the only thing that matters. So, we need to train ourselves to see it, act on it, and make sure our lives are rooted in it. When fear comes, and it will, you won't be left scrambling for something to hold onto. You'll already be standing on solid ground.

Takeaway

The demonic tactic of fostering irrational fear and passivity opposes God's will for us. "Fear everything" is the devil's message, while "Don't be afraid" is God's. You must make a conscious choice about how to live your life. God, through the prophet Isaiah, promises us, "So don't be afraid, for I am with you; do not be dismayed for I am your God. I will strengthen you and help you; I will uphold you with my righteous right hand."

The life-changing truth here is that you don't have to let fear run your life, ever again. Fear will always try to speak, but it doesn't get to be the final voice. Every time you choose courage rooted in God's presence rather than the lies of "what if," you break chains the enemy has tried to tighten around your heart. God hasn't promised a life without valleys, but He has promised to walk with you through them. When you decide to face today's real challenges with faith instead of surrendering to tomorrow's imagined fears, something shifts inside you: your spirit strengthens, your trust deepens, and fear begins to lose its grip.

This is your invitation to live differently. You don't have to wait for fear to disappear; you can act boldly in the middle of it, knowing that God's power is greater than your anxiety. Each courageous step, however small, is a declaration that you belong to Him, not to your fears. Over time, this choice rewires your heart to trust God more deeply, allowing peace and strength to replace panic and doubt. Your fear can become the very ground where your faith grows unshakable.

A Closing Prayer

Lord, I pray that you would guard my heart and mind in Christ Jesus. I pray that you will give me clarity to know when and how to act in the face of things that make me fearful or anxious. I ask you to strengthen my mind, build my faith, and impassion my heart to walk through life fearing nothing but you. Give me wisdom to know the cross you have given me to bear and the strength to pick it up daily. In Jesus' name, Amen!

Chapter 7
The Error of Extremes

The demonic prefer to work quietly, subtly, from the shadows. They exploit our vulnerabilities, our emotions, and our good intentions. They whisper half-truths and plant small seeds of division. They don't need to destroy the church with a frontal assault when they can simply get us fighting each other from within. One of the most effective tools in Satan's arsenal is taking something good in us, like passion for truth or love for God, and slowly turning it into something divisive. He nudges us toward extremes. He fans the flames of our strongest beliefs until they become obsessions. Before we know it, we're more concerned with defending our position than loving our neighbor, more focused on being right than being Christlike. Let's explore how Satan operates in the details, and how we can resist his subtle sabotage.

Scripture

"Who shall ascend the hill of the Lord, And who shall stand in his holy place? He who has clean hands and a pure heart, who does not lift up his soul to what is false and does not swear deceitfully. He will receive blessing from the Lord and righteousness from the God of his salvation." - Psalm 24:3-5

Overt or Covert Manipulation

Satan rarely shows up with horns and a pitchfork. There's no dramatic showdown, no head-spinning possession, no voice from the darkness announcing evil's arrival. That would be too obvious. If Satan fully revealed himself and his schemes, people would wake up to the reality of spiritual warfare and run to church. So instead, he works quietly, patiently, and strategically.

Think about how this plays out in everyday life. The demonic don't need to drag you into some dark ritual to pull you away from God. They can do it through much simpler means: a nagging insecurity that grows into bitterness, a political conviction that hardens into self-righteousness, a theological preference that becomes a litmus test for fellowship. Satan exploits our emotions, our pride, our desire to be right. He takes our strengths and slowly twists them into weaknesses.

Lewis captures this brilliantly in Letters 7. The goal isn't to make people deny spiritual realities altogether. That's too hard for Satan to pull off. Most people sense there's something beyond the physical world. Instead, the demonic strategy is to foster vague, undefined spirituality. Keep people "spiritual" without ever getting specific about God, sin, salvation, or Jesus. Convince them that all paths lead to the same place, that sincerity matters more than truth, that feelings trump doctrine. They love it when we talk about "the universe" having a plan, when we say we're "spiritual but not religious." Whether it's yoga mysticism, Christian Science, self-help gurus, or the "coexist" bumper sticker on *Karen's* car. Satan has thousands of ways for mankind to pursue some level of spirituality while keeping us blind to the truth.

This is why Scripture tells us that true worshipers must worship God in spirit AND in truth (John 4:24). Both matter. Spirit without truth becomes empty mysticism. Truth without spirit becomes dead religion. The demonic are content with either extreme, as long as we never find the living God who demands both our hearts and our minds.

The danger for Christians isn't that we'll stop believing in God. It's that we'll start believing in the wrong things about Him, or that we'll elevate secondary issues to primary importance. Satan doesn't need to attack the church from the outside if he can get us tearing it apart from within. And he does this through quiet manipulation: ideologies that sound reasonable, emotional impulses that feel justified, and divisions that seem necessary for the sake of truth.

This letter reminds us that we must be discerning. There is a real spiritual war going on, and it thrives when we are kept at bay with half-truths leading to whole mistakes in our understanding of the world and our role in shaping it.

The Danger of Ideological Extremes

During World War II, when Lewis wrote *The Screwtape Letters*, British Christians faced a specific dilemma, would they be disarmed into embracing total pacifism or deceived to pursuing extreme patriotism? Lewis saw how demons could use either extreme to pull believers away from their purpose.

We've touched on the problem of these extremes earlier, but here we need to dig deeper into how this plays out specifically within the church. It's one thing to recognize that the world pushes us toward extreme positions. It's another to see how easily those same patterns infiltrate our faith communities and poison them from within.

The demonic love to tempt us toward passionate causes. These are things that promise purpose, identity, and righteousness: a political movement, a theological position, a cultural battle, a denominational loyalty. None of these things are inherently bad. In fact, many are good, and we need to engage in these areas. But when any cause becomes ultimate, when it dethrones Christ from the center, it becomes a tool of division.

The devil doesn't care which extreme you run toward, as long as you abandon the narrow road of faithful obedience. He's equally content with a mind consumed by theological pride or cultural rage, political activism, or an emphasis on "staying in our lane." What matters to him is that you're off balance. And the more passionately you cling to your chosen extreme, the more likely you are to isolate yourself from other believers and justify it as righteousness.

Here's where it gets tricky. Christians are called to speak truth and stand firm. We're supposed to have convictions. And we are to walk in authority, being salt and light. But Lewis warns us against the error of treating temporal causes as spiritual absolutes. When we allow a secondary issue to become our defining mark, we risk turning the means into the end. Our faith should overflow into every aspect of our lives, including politics and social issues. But it's so easy to get the wires crossed. Rather than letting our faith shape our worldview, we can allow our worldview to corrupt our faith.

Ask yourself this, is this conviction helping me love God and love my neighbor more deeply, or is it just making me more angry, tribal, and self-righteous? If you find yourself holding a political or social or theological belief a little too tightly, you might want to pause and let the Lord examine your heart. It may be best to ease up a little and give it to the Lord to adjust your perspective and heart.

Navigating Unity and Truth

The challenge of maintaining biblical unity while holding fast to truth requires discernment and wisdom. Scripture calls us to "contend for the faith" (Jude 1:3) while also pursuing "the unity of the Spirit in the bond of peace" (Ephesians 4:3). This tension isn't a contradiction to resolve but a balance to maintain.

Consider how Paul addressed the Corinthian church's divisions. When believers declared "I follow Paul" or "I follow Apollos," they weren't debating doctrine but pledging allegiance to personalities. Paul's correction was swift, such factionalism betrayed a fundamental misunderstanding of the gospel's unifying power. Christ cannot be divided, and neither should His body fracture over preferences.

The subtlety of this error makes it particularly dangerous. Our motivations often begin nobly, we desire doctrinal purity, biblical fidelity, and uncompromising truth. Yet without careful guard over our hearts, conviction morphs into condescension, discernment becomes suspicion, and zeal transforms into zealotry. The very passion meant to protect the faith becomes a weapon that wounds the faithful.

I love the message behind Psalm 24, as it helps us address how we should set our hearts. It describes those who may ascend the Lord's hill as having "clean hands and a pure heart," not perfection, but humility coupled with sincere pursuit of righteousness.

To help walk this balance, there's a helpful framework that my pastor often used for identifying which issues in life we should hold more closely than others. I've heard many others teach it in a similar way. He refers to it as open-hand and closed-hand issues. Looking at it this way helps us preserve unity without sacrificing truth when discerning challenging issues. And the principle is also helpful in making sure unhealthy extremes don't become central or divisive.

Closed-hand issues are the non-negotiables of life or faith. These are the core doctrines that define Christianity. We would put issues like the authority and inerrancy of Scripture, the divinity of Jesus Christ, His atoning death and resurrection, and the exclusive nature of salvation through Him in the closed hand. We can't budge on these issues without compromising fundamental truth and reality. These truths must be held tightly. To loosen our grip on these essentials is to unravel the gospel itself.

Open-hand issues, however, are those matters over which sincere believers may disagree. These include worship style, denominational governance, and secondary theological interpretations like perspectives on baptism or eschatology (how and when Jesus is coming back). These topics are important, but they are not ultimate. When we treat open-hand issues like closed-hand doctrines, we sow division, create factions, and fall into the error of extremes. Wisdom in life is knowing which issues belong in which hand.

Takeaway

In every generation, Satan tailors his strategy to the times. Today, he leverages distraction, division, and distortion. He entices us to trade gospel clarity for tribal allegiance. He wins when we confuse our political or theological preferences with ultimate truth. He wins when we spend more time defending our camp than proclaiming the kingdom. The solution is not disengagement, but discernment. We need courage without contempt. Conviction without cruelty. Boldness without blindness. We must keep our heads down in obedience and diligence, but also lift them up in reflection, compassion, and worship. Eyes on Christ. Hands open to correction. Hearts anchored in truth. As

Lewis writes, "Once you have made the world an end, and faith a means, you have almost won your man." Let us not be men and women who weaponize faith to serve our ends. Let us be those who follow Christ with clean hands, pure hearts, and an unwavering gaze fixed on the things that are true and matter most.

A Closing Prayer

Heavenly Father, Help me to walk in Your light all the days of my life. Keep my heart free from idols and guard me from placing any worldly ideas or desires above You. Grant me discernment as I read and live out Your Word. Keep me from pride, from self-righteousness, and from twisting truth to serve myself. Let my obedience to Christ be genuine and humble as I seek to love and serve those around me in truth. In Jesus' name, Amen.

Chapter 8
The Law of Undulation

Life is not a constant state of being but a rhythmic journey of peaks and valleys. Life is not a flat line but a dynamic cadence filled with twists and turns. We move over mountaintops and through valleys, experience joy and pain, intimacy with God, and times of distance. C. S. Lewis calls this the "Law of Undulation," and once you accept this premise as the way life is and should be, it is revelatory, life-changing, and freedom-giving. It changes how you view every season of life. This concept is central to *The Screwtape Letters,* and it's one we'll return to throughout this book. In this chapter, we'll explore what undulation really is, how God uses it to shape us, and how we should respond when we find ourselves in one of those deep spiritual troughs.

Scripture

"I know how to be brought low, and I know how to abound. In any and every circumstance, I have learned the secret of facing plenty and hunger, abundance and need. I can do all things through him who strengthens me." - Philippians 4:12–13

What Is Undulation?

I think of undulation like sound waves, a repeating pattern of peaks and valleys. That variation of high and low is what gives the sound its tone and energy. Remove the variation, and all you're left with is flat silence. Or picture a ship riding the stormy ocean. It moves through the water, lifting on the crests and sinking into the troughs, repeating the process over and over again on its journey.

Life mirrors this motion in many ways. If you think about it, virtually every aspect of life will ebb and flow along the way. Relationships, emotions, work, finances, sports teams, the stock market, and even the weather has a natural cadence of highs and lows. And of course, one way we experience the law of undulation is in our walk with the Lord. One moment, we feel close to God, spiritually alive and thriving; the next, we find ourselves in dry spells, spiritual confusion, or suffering. We experience seasons where we feel we are growing, learning, and excited. And other times when we feel stagnant, empty, and depressed. That's undulation.

The Law of Undulation describes the natural rhythm of human life. The rise and fall of our emotional, spiritual, and physical states. As beings that are both physical and spiritual, we are also not static. We fluctuate as we're subject to the world as God designed it. We are built for eternity, but bound by the created order, making us highly susceptible to the natural occurrence of highs and lows.

We see this law throughout Scripture. Think of King David, for example, he was chosen and anointed by God but still struggled with his faith through the peaks and valleys.

We see in Psalm 21:1-2 David singing of God's goodness and tangible presence, "O Lord, in your strength the king rejoices, and in your salvation how greatly he exults! You have given him his heart's desire and have not withheld the request of his lips." But in the very next Psalm, we see what seems to be the complete opposite. In Psalm 22:1-2, he says, "My God, My God, why have You forsaken Me? Why are You so far from helping Me, And from the words of My groaning? O My God, I cry in the daytime, but You do not hear; And in the night season, and am not silent." Talk about a 180!

Undulation is a natural cycle that happens to the best and the worst of us. But we often fail to recognize that. The Enemy exploits our ignorance of this principle. He wants us to believe that spiritual lows mean failure, or even abandonment. He wants us to expect life to be a constant high so that when it's not, we despair. But that's a lie. This pattern is not a bug in the system. It's a feature. It's how growth happens. Only a fool, or someone who doesn't accept God's dominion over us, would expect the good times to last forever. All the time, we hear about singers, actors, or other celebrities filing for bankruptcy after spending as if their income would never change. What a humbling feeling and sober reminder that nothing on this earth is constant, except God. But not only are the low times in life not something that should lead to despair. As we'll see in the rest of this chapter, the troughs are not evidence of God's absence. They're often where He is doing His deepest work.

How God Uses the Valleys

The low seasons are not wasted in God's economy. Times of loss, suffering, doubt, discouragement, or silence are not detours from the Christian journey; they are often the very terrain where faith is refined. When life feels like a trough, Satan will try to use it to pull us toward cynicism. He'll whisper that our faith was just a phase, a "honeymoon period," "Your God has abandoned you," or something we've outgrown. He wants us to see our present dryness as proof that we were naïve to believe in the first place. But God uses the very same season to draw us nearer to Himself.

When we are in a low season, the unchanging character of God comes into sharper focus. He becomes the steady point on the horizon, the fortress that will not fall, the rock that will not move. Scripture calls Him a strong tower, a refuge in times of trouble. In those moments, His lovingkindness and faithfulness are not abstract theological ideas but are the lifeline we cling to. David understood this when he wrote in Psalm 23:4, "Even though I walk through the valley of the shadow of death, I will fear no evil, for You are with me." At the same time, the enemy will work to convince us that despair is the only logical conclusion, or that pleasure, distraction, or outright denial of God will bring relief. But this is simply another form of enslavement. In those moments, we are faced with a clear choice, follow the enemy's lure into bondage or draw closer to the God who never changes.

Another way God uses the valleys is by turning them into powerful stories of redemption. Job's suffering was not the result of personal wrongdoing, yet he lost his wealth, his health, and his children in rapid succession. His grief was deep, and his questions were raw, but his conclusion was resolute, "Though He slay me, yet will I trust Him" (Job 13:15). And in the end, God restored Job and revealed His purposes. The story stands as a reminder that suffering is not always a sign of God's displeasure but can be the stage for His glory and the deepening of our faith.

Or consider Jesus on the cross. As He hung there, He cried out the opening words of Psalm 22, "My God, my God, why have You forsaken me?" If anyone ever knew what it meant to walk through the valley, it was the Son of God in that moment. His suffering was not a meaningless tragedy. It was the very means by which salvation was accomplished. What looked like the enemy's greatest victory became his ultimate defeat. If God can redeem the cross, He can redeem any valley we face.

God uses the valleys to grow our faith and character. Times when we are weary, spiritually dry, or struggling to focus on Him. Others are the painful realities of living in a sin-cursed world: illness, loss, betrayal, or hardship. Still others may be the direct consequences of our own actions. Sometimes our valleys are self-inflicted, the result of sin, poor decisions, or foolishness. King David experienced this when his adultery and murder brought profound consequences upon his life and family (2 Samuel 11-12). But even in those moments, the law of undulation still applies. God can redeem what we've broken and use our failures as the very ground where repentance, humility, and restoration take root. But in every case, God can use them to test our faith, refine our character, and deepen our reliance on Him.

It's in the valley that we learn obedience that isn't driven by emotion or convenience. We pray when the words feel empty. We worship when the feelings aren't there. We keep walking when the path is unclear. That kind of faith is forged in the fire and cannot be manufactured in times of ease. Just as showing up to work on a hard morning builds discipline, showing up for God in a dry season builds spiritual endurance. This is the steadying power of undulation, the highs lift us, the lows strengthen us, and both are essential to the Christian life.

Staying Faithful in the Lows

Recognizing a trough for what it is changes how we move through it. If we expect life to be a constant high, we'll see the valley as a failure or a punishment. But if we accept undulation as part of God's design, we can respond with wisdom rather than with despair. Here are a few helpful ways to navigate the troughs.

Stay Spiritually Engaged

Low seasons tempt us to pull back from prayer, Scripture, worship, and fellowship, waiting until we "feel it" again. That's the moment we most need to press in. Spiritual disciplines are not dependent on emotion. They are lifelines in the dry places. The habits formed in easier times become anchors in the hard ones.

Fill Your Mind with Truth

In times like these, we are especially vulnerable to false conclusions: that God has turned away from us, that our faith was just a phase, or that pleasure and self-reliance are better options. These thoughts may feel reasonable in the moment but are nothing more than chains. We must be intentional about filling our minds with God's truth through Scripture, godly counsel, and reminders of His character. We want the truth, we know it can carry us when feelings falter. God is faithful, loving, kind, just, forgiving, longsuffering, and redeeming.

Stay Active

The trough is not a place to remain idle. Even small actions can break the inertia. Sometimes, just doing the next right thing, handling one part of a problem, or simply starting the day with purpose can provide hope and help turn the tide. This includes staying connected to others. Low seasons often isolate us, pulling us away from church, community groups, and friendships. Even serving others and staying plugged in can shift our perspective, remind us we're not alone, and help us see God at work in ways we might otherwise miss. Just stay active in doing good!

Undulation is inevitable. The question is not whether we will face valleys, but how we will walk through them. When we persevere, we emerge stronger, more rooted, and more aware of the God who was with us every step of the way.

The story of Horatio Spafford, who wrote the hymn "It Is Well With My Soul" after losing his family in a shipwreck, is a testament to staying true to God through the hard times, a testament to finding peace amidst profound pain. This underscores the belief that one can respond to tragedy with either bitterness or growth and that maintaining faith during challenging times can be transformative.

Takeaway

Undulation is not a flaw in the system. It is the system. It's the rhythm of spiritual life. And the key to navigating it is not to resist the motion but to remain faithful within it. God uses the peaks to renew us and the troughs to refine us. He's not distant in your dry season. He's at work in ways you may not see until later. The demonic will whisper that your suffering proves God has left you. Don't believe it. The valley is where God forms sons and daughters who trust Him even in the dark.

So, whether you're riding high or walking low, stay the course. Don't confuse God's silence for His absence. Don't mistake emotional distance for spiritual defeat. Keep praying. Keep worshiping. Keep obeying. The law of undulation is a fact of life. But it's also a doorway to deeper faith.

A Closing Prayer

My Lord, forgive me for my unfaithfulness in times of trouble, when I walk through valleys and cannot sense You near. Forgive me for when I stand on the peaks of life's joys and forget that I am there only because of You. Too often, I have placed my reliance on the world ahead of my trust in You. Forgive me. Help me not lean on my own understanding but fully submit my life to You. You are the Good

Shepherd. Strengthen my faith and help me listen for Your guidance. With praise and worship, I will sing hallelujah all the days of my life. Amen!

Chapter 9
Satan in the Trough Seasons

In the last letter, we explored how God uses the valleys of life to refine us, strengthen our faith, and deepen our reliance on Him. The troughs are not wasted seasons. They're where God does some of His most important work. But there's another side to this story. While God is redeeming the valley, Satan is exploiting it. The same low season that draws us closer to God can also make us vulnerable to the enemy's most destructive temptations and perversions.

When we find ourselves in the dark seasons of life, the flesh becomes susceptible to quick, destructive remedies. Alcohol, drugs, pornography, and other numbing agents beckon like sirens, promising relief but delivering only a hollow echo of shameful satisfaction. These are the traps laid carefully by the demonic, designed to exploit our most fragile emotional states. The devil's tactics in the trough differ from the ones he uses in our spiritual peaks. This chapter will look squarely at the ways these low seasons open us up to attack, how Satan distorts God's good gifts, and how we can choose to respond with godly perspective and truth.

> *"Watch and pray that you may not enter into temptation. The spirit indeed is willing, but the flesh is weak." -*
> *Matthew 26:41*

The Vulnerability of the Trough

When explaining the golden opportunity Wormwood has to capitalize on the patient's low season, Screwtape lays out a clear principle, "(Demonic) attack has a much better chance of success when the man's whole inner world is drab, cold, and empty." The reason is simple, when we're struggling, our defenses are down. Whatever is causing the trough (illness, financial stress, grief, family conflict) much of our energy is consumed just getting through the day. Like an infantry unit with scattered resources, we find ourselves weak and exposed. These are the moments when our shield of faith is compromised.

This is when the battle shifts to the mind. Satan floods us with lies and discouraging thoughts, creating a fog of confusion. With our guard down and energy depleted, we start believing distortions, "Life will always be this way… I thought my faith was supposed to be elevating… I must have messed something up… now it's going to be depressing forever." Rather than recognizing the trough as a passing season, we believe our previous joy was the phase and it's gone for good. We might even hear Scripture as an indictment rather than encouragement, "If you faint in the day of adversity, your strength is small" (Prov. 24:10).

The demonic know we're weary, drained, and hurting. They know we're more inclined to chase quick relief than to take the slower path of faithfulness. We begin looking for anything to alleviate the pain: quick hits of dopamine, immediate comfort, escape. Our judgment becomes compromised. The physical and mental duress leads us to do and think things we otherwise wouldn't. And the enemy is ready with his arsenal of false comforts like sexual sin, substance abuse, bitterness, and isolation. The very pleasures God designed for good become twisted into traps. We're vulnerable, and Satan knows it.

Perverting God's Pleasures

All pleasure belongs to God. He designed all things good and gave them to man to enjoy with thanksgiving. Satan, on the other hand, has no pleasures of his own. Lewis even quips that the demonic "research" hasn't resulted in creating even a single joy. All the demonic can do then is take the pleasures that God created and cause us to distort and pervert, so we miss the joy intended for us.

The word "perversion" often brings to mind a certain stereotype. The sexual deviant, the peeping tom, the guy who always and only has a dirty joke on hand. But the term is far broader than a "creep." Perversion means to take something good, clean, and pure and twist it into something ugly, harmful, and unclean. Like the warped mirrors in a carnival funhouse, the original image is still there but distorted beyond recognition. This is perversion. And it's how Satan treats all of God's good gifts. Sex, food, drink, wealth, and rest, all designed by God, can all be twisted into slavery, addiction, and destruction.

The trough season is when we are most vulnerable to these demonic perversions. Let's look at some of the most common pitfalls in our time.

The Sensual Temptations

Sex is a gift from God, designed for joy, intimacy, and covenant love. In peak seasons, healthy sexuality is directed toward our spouse in life-giving ways. But in low seasons, our loneliness, depression, and pain make us more likely to seek out false intimacy. We become more inclined to do things we wouldn't otherwise do.

My pastor would say that he believes only two kinds of men don't struggle with sexual temptation: "Dead men and liars." And as a man, I have to agree. Low times can be particularly dangerous for falling into sexual sin, especially "unnatural debased sexual things" like pornography. People are more likely to engage in these behaviors when depressed or in emotional distress. In these moments, we find ourselves looking for any possible way to dull the pain or find emotional relief.

Globally, today's pornography world is pumping out content at a fast clip. It is no longer merely a dark aspect of the Hollywood industry; it has now expanded globally. Not only is the content more accessible, but it is also more graphic, violent, and varied in ways that men of yesteryear could only have imagined, or one might have prayed would never be real. Pornography doesn't just corrupt the consumer; it also corrupts those influenced into participating in the industry. In dark times, when men lean into pornography, it creates a demand. Producers see the demand and respond by creating more extreme content and by recruiting more vulnerable men and women into the industry. Any consumption is, in effect, an investment in the porn industry. Sexuality that is so grossly perverted has man is searching for joy, meaning, connection, and pleasure, often due to the fact that a trough season is bringing pain and suffering.

Alcohol

Drinking is another good gift God designed to be received with joy and thanksgiving. Scripture affirms that "all things are to be received with gratefulness." Wine gladdens the heart (Psalm 104:15) and Jesus Himself turned water into wine at Cana. But in the trough, the enemy distorts this gift from celebration into coping and eventually vice.

Alcohol is an accelerant to the "fuddled" state we discussed in Letter 1. Once fuddled, mankind makes terrible, regretful choices. The joy and merriment that God designed for us are often overpromised when it comes to alcohol. And people who are desperate for relief end up looking for that joy so feverishly that a blessing is quickly perverted into a vice. And when it comes to substance, the cycle continues, and the need for joy increases, and perverted pleasures deliver less and less. Lewis understood a critical psychological mechanism; the pursuit of temporary pleasure creates an ever-increasing craving for an ever-diminishing reward. Each attempt to escape pain through these mechanisms spirals downward, creating a vortex that pulls individuals deeper into despair. The dopamine hit becomes smaller, while the emptiness becomes larger.

The destruction that comes from these empty pursuits impacts so many areas of life. Think for a moment about the number of abortions that happen because of drunken nights, or the crimes, including sex crimes, exacerbated by intoxication. Talk about examples of wins for the demonic. Imagine a demon's delight in convincing a woman to destroy the life God has created in her womb, while also scarring her soul.

In the trough, it's easier to reach for the bottle than for your Bible. Pray for light in this dark place and know that God will not abandon you.

Drugs

Medical advancement is part of humanity's dominion mandate. God gave us the created order and called us to steward it, refine it, and use it for good. We take compounds from creation and turn them into tools that alleviate suffering. Painkillers like morphine or fentanyl, when used as designed, are profound gifts that allow surgeons to operate and patients to recover. Hospitals bear witness to this calling, often being named after saints, denominations, or biblical themes. Even the symbol on the ambulance, the serpent on the staff, comes from Numbers 21, where those who looked upon it would be healed. God is for healing.

But in the trough, the enemy takes this gift and twists it into devastation. Fentanyl, designed to ease surgical pain, has become one of the deadliest street drugs in America. People desperate for relief turn to substances that promise escape but deliver enslavement. Drug abuse doesn't just harm the body; it defaces the image of God. Look at someone addicted to methamphetamine, a once-vibrant face becomes hollowed out, aged beyond recognition. Nothing distorts the human image quite like addiction.

The trough makes us vulnerable to this perversion. When we're hurting with no end in sight, instant relief becomes irresistible. But what starts as pain management becomes pain multiplication. God designed medicine to heal. Satan uses it to destroy.

The Choice of Perspective

As we said earlier, the trough season becomes a battle of the mind. A demonic fog of war. And Screwtape makes a very interesting statement to Wormwood in this letter. He says, "The first step is to keep knowledge out of his mind. Do not let him suspect the law of undulation."

C. S. Lewis grew up in a Christian home but abandoned faith as a young man, calling himself an atheist. For years, he followed intellectual pride, cynicism, and a restless search for pleasure and meaning, but he later described feeling "pushed" by unseen forces toward despair and self-destruction.

In his autobiography *Surprised by Joy*, Lewis wrote that he eventually recognized something *spiritual* was at play, not merely psychological struggle, or bad luck. He called it "the shadowed road," where he began to realize there were influences pulling him away from truth, joy, and goodness.

At one point, he said it felt as if there was a battle for his mind and will, that the darkness wasn't just within him, but something whispering lies and keeping him chained to self-centered thinking. That realization, that there was an intelligent evil resisting his change, was his moment of awakening. Once he named that force and turned toward God, he described it as "being pulled back from a dark, wild sea into the safety of shore."

That recognition, that he wasn't merely weak, but under spiritual attack, gave him the perspective and strength to fight back. He called that the start of his healing and his climb toward faith and freedom. He remarked, "When I actually realized that it was a demonic force influencing me to make terrible decisions, I was awakened to the strategy pressing on me and became able to start healing and climbing out of the trough."

Ultimately, resilience emerges from a deliberate choice. Acknowledge the pain, feel its weight, but refuse to be consumed. Cultivate gratitude, even in microscopic doses. Understand that emotional maturity is not about eliminating darkness but about choosing light while also fully experiencing the shadows. Gratitude can be a powerful tool in rewiring one's mental state. The key is to be realistic about challenges while choosing to remain positive and proactive. Yes, choosing to remain positive, true, and purposeful can be tough instead of being impatient and impetuous. It is the only choice when your goal is to push through the valley and return to the peak.

Scripture commands us to guard our hearts and minds in Christ Jesus. I think this is especially important in the trough seasons. Watch out for attacks on your faith directly, where the enemy will convince you, your faith was a phase, tempting you to think, "I was probably too excited about the Jesus stuff." Satan will also nurture cynicism and intellectualism to try to rationalize suffering and pain without God's wisdom. It's amazing how a difficult season can pervert faith and make someone cold and haughty when, in reality, their air of superiority is nothing more than a coping mechanism they developed rather than seeking the Lord through the valley.

Takeaway

The key to navigating these low periods is to be intentional about redirecting energy toward positive activities such as meaningful work, productive thinking, or "innocuous merriment." This approach can help break negative cycles and potentially lead to personal growth. The low times are not moments to feel sorry for yourself but to grind, dig deep in your character, and work your way out of this. Surround yourself with a support group that can help you stay on track, hold you accountable, and guide you forward. Finding this amongst men of faith or "Experienced Christians," as Lewis puts it, is even better, as they can also pray for and with you. The power of prayer can never be underestimated, as petitioning God can render powerful results, and He will protect you in the trough.

Closing Prayer

Lord, thank You for being the God of the mountains and the God of the valleys. Help me and protect me, especially during the seasons of life when I am struggling and feel farthest from You. Forgive me of my sin, heal me from my shame, and strengthen me in the power of Your might. Help me to return to joy and always worship You in all things. In Jesus name, Amen.

Chapter 10
Fear of Man and the Double Life

The modern Christian life is often a delicate dance of integrity, a constant negotiation between personal conviction and social pressure. Letter 10 gives us an uncomfortably accurate picture of how friendships and social environments can shape our character, not by open hostility to the faith, but through small, almost invisible compromises.

We've all been there. The coworker makes a joke that mocks something you believe, and instead of speaking up, you force a laugh. Your friends plan something for Sunday morning, and instead of saying you go to church, you make up an excuse. Someone asks what you did over the weekend, and you mention everything except the worship service that meant the world to you. These small moments of silence don't feel like betrayals at the time, but they do issue compromise. In the quiet corners of offices, social gatherings, and casual conversations, a spiritual battle unfolds. Before long, the self we are in church and the self we are in the world become two different people entirely.

Scripture

"The fear of man lays a snare, but whoever trusts in the Lord is safe." - Proverbs 29:25

Fear of Man

The fear of man is the root of countless compromises. It can make us passive when we should be active, and active when we should be passive, what we call "crossing the wires." Lewis captures this reversal perfectly, the Patient will "laugh when he should be silent" and "be silent when he should speak." Sometimes this looks like affirming a crude joke with a chuckle when our conscience winces. Other times, it's saying nothing when God's truth is openly mocked, out of fear that we'll be labeled intolerant or self-righteous.

One of the highest callings of a man is to not fear another. This is not a small thing or a trivial pursuit. The fear of man versus the fear of God is one of the defining battles of the human soul. It determines whether we live as slaves to the shifting opinions of others or as free men and women accountable only to our Creator. To resist the fear of man is to pursue virtue at its highest level. It is to walk in freedom, integrity, and courage. And yet, this noble calling is tested not in grand moments of heroism, but in the small, daily compromises that slowly reshape who we are.

Fear of man works not only through our words, but also through subtle cues, a nod that signals agreement when we don't actually agree. Remaining in a conversation we know we should exit. Choosing comfort over conviction in a moment that matters. It is important to recognize how public opinion, workplace relationships, and friend groups can gradually shift one's spiritual perspective and even have us equivocating on big issues.

In the workplace, fear of man is particularly potent. I've worked for organizations where the open celebration of faith in Jesus would be considered inappropriate, even as other religious or ideological celebrations were encouraged. I've turned the corner in an office to find a Muslim colleague on a prayer mat, a Sikh wearing a turban, and a coworker wearing pride-themed attire, all without consequence. Yet for a Christian to share openly about their faith could invite discomfort, awkward questions, or even disapproval from leadership.

These situations reveal an important reality; the enemy doesn't need to destroy our faith outright; he only needs to convince us it's safer to hide it. Proverbs 29:25 warns us that the fear of man lays a snare, and snares rarely look like traps until they've already tightened.

The Quiet Corruption of Friendship

Show me your friends and I'll show you your future. This isn't just a catchy saying. It's a spiritual reality. Lewis's Patient surrounds himself with people whose values are rooted in vanity, skepticism, and worldliness. They aren't necessarily overtly hostile to Christianity; they simply live as if it doesn't matter. And over time, their gravitational pull erodes the sharp edges of his convictions.

Here's what we often miss: your friendships as a whole have more impact on you than you have on all of your friendships combined. You might think you can be the strong influence, the one who changes the group, but more often than not, the group changes you. We begin to endorse ungodly ideas, not with deliberate statements, but through body language, laughter, or the absence of protest. This is how "bad company corrupts good morals" (1 Cor. 15:33).

Sometimes the corruption is so gradual we barely notice it. Early in my walk with Christ, I worked construction sites where faith was a punchline and vulgarity were the native language. I didn't set out to compromise, but slowly, my speech, humor, and attitudes shifted. I was still "a Christian," but I was also fitting in just fine with a crew whose values were far from Christlike. That subtle drift is exactly what Lewis warns about.

Think about your own friendships. Not everyone needs to be at the same level of spiritual maturity, but ask yourself, are there people in your inner circle who are pulling you away from God? Friendships aren't equal. There are casual acquaintances, and then there are the people who have real influence over your decisions, your mindset, and your character. If someone in that inner circle is consistently leading you toward compromise, it may be time to create some distance. Move them to an outer circle. It's not about rejection or judgment. It's about protecting your character.

Friendships can be one of the greatest blessings of life, but it can also be a slow-acting poison if our closest bonds lead us away from God. Give yourself grace for past failures in this area, but don't stay passive. Take action. Evaluate who has access to your heart and your habits. Because the people you walk with will determine the direction you go.

The Double Life and Its Dangers

Lewis describes a man who leads two separate lives, one with his Christian friends, another with his non-Christian companions, each version carefully shaped to fit in. This is not just the perception of a double life; it is reality because when we genuinely try to play both sides, we craft two versions of ourselves. Around Christians, we appear spiritually mature and committed. But with others, we hide our faith completely, keeping things surface-level. We try to please everyone, while ultimately letting everyone down. Our Christian friends only see part of who we are, while others never know what we truly believe. Fear of man overrides faithfulness to God, leaving us unfaithful not only to the Lord but to ourselves. This double life produces a divided heart, unstable, conflicted, and unable to commit fully to either path.

I've lived some of this tension myself. In younger years, I could be one man in a Sunday worship setting and another on a Friday night. My church friends might have been shocked by my language or the jokes I laughed at during the week; my coworkers might have rolled their eyes if I had openly lived my faith. The discomfort wasn't just about fear of their opinions; it was the realization that there was a discrepancy in my character, and I didn't want to face it.

This is the hidden cost of the double life, not only the instability it breeds, but the erosion of integrity until we no longer know which "self" is real. Worse, we convince ourselves we're sophisticated enough to manage both worlds. But James 1:8 cuts through the delusion, "A double-minded man is unstable in all his ways." You cannot serve two masters. Eventually, the split will break you.

Integrity and Character

The antidote to fear of man and double-minded living is character. Character means being the same person everywhere. It's not about forcing conversations about faith into every interaction. It's about never betraying truth to maintain comfort. Integrity is about consistency.

Integrity and character mean that what you present to the world is actually who you are on the inside. The person you are with one friend group is the same person you are with another. The person you are in public is the same person you are in private. What you say you'll do is what you actually do. This kind of character is only possible when you stop seeking the approval of man and start seeking only the approval of God.

You cannot have true integrity if you fear man. The two cannot coexist. When you care more about the opinions of others than you do about obedience to God, consistency becomes impossible. You'll always be adjusting, performing, and hiding parts of yourself to fit in. But when your allegiance is to Christ alone, integrity becomes natural. You don't have to remember what version of yourself you're supposed to be because there's only one version. When we live chained to the opinions of others, we forfeit the freedom Christ died to give us. True liberty begins when we stop seeking approval from people and start walking in the identity God has given us.

Being courageous in expressing Christian beliefs doesn't come without a response from the world, but faith becomes your breastplate of righteousness. Sometimes courage means walking away from certain social circles. Other times it means staying and speaking gentle truth when the moment calls for it. If you feel rejected because of your faith, dust off your feet and move on. Don't become what others want you to be just to fit in. If people won't accept you for who you are in Christ, why would you want them to accept you for something you're not?

Modern life offers countless arenas for compromise: workplaces, online spaces, social gatherings. In corporate environments, Diversity, Equity, and Inclusion initiatives can create unspoken rules about what's acceptable to express. Religious diversity is celebrated in theory, but in practice, Christianity often becomes the one belief expected to remain silent. While it's wise to navigate these waters with tact, the call to integrity remains, do not allow the world to dictate which parts of your faith are safe to display.

Here's your challenge, identify areas of your life where you've compromised your integrity. Where have you cared more about the opinions of man than the truth of God? Where have you given in to peer pressure, laughed at jokes your conscience rejected, or stayed silent when you should have spoken? Name those moments. Confess them. And then make a decision to live differently.

This is where courage is contagious. One believer's quiet consistency can give others permission to do the same, even in environments that seem hostile to Christ. When we stand up, others often step up and join us. It begins with a simple yet profound commitment, being the same person everywhere. And as Proverbs reminds us, trusting in the Lord is the only safe place to stand when the pressure mounts. Don't live in fear of man. Live in fear of God alone. That is where freedom, integrity, and true courage are found.

Takeaway

As we walk consistently with Christ, the divide between "church self" and "work self" begins to dissolve. The transformation is subtle but profound, less about aggressive proclamation and more about quiet, consistent authenticity. Faithfulness is rarely tested in public moments; it's forged in the quiet, daily choices of integrity. Fear of man will always lay a snare, but trust in the Lord will keep us safe. Whether in friendships, the workplace, or family life, our calling is the same, be one person, wholly devoted to Christ, wherever we are. The most powerful testimony is not found in grand declarations but in the quiet, unwavering consistency of a life truly aligned with Christ.

A Closing Prayer

Dear Lord Jesus, guard me against the pressure that would draw me away from You. Fill me with the Holy Spirit to guide and strengthen me. Help me never to compromise my faith out of fear of what others think. Let me speak Your name boldly, without being controlled by human approval. Help me grow friendships rooted in faith and walk authentically as a follower of Christ, humble and hungry for You. Grant me the courage to carry my faith in every aspect of my life. Strengthen me through trials, protect me from failing, and empower me to resist all attacks of the enemy in Your name. Amen.

Chapter 11
Redeeming Humor

In Letter 11, C. S. Lewis describes four kinds of laughter. At the top is Joy, then Fun, then the Joke Proper, and finally Flippancy. This is not a list of morally neutral categories. Joy is pure and godly. Romans 5:5 says, "Real joy comes from God, who has invaded us, conquered us, and liberated us from eternal death and sadness." Flippancy is the most debased and spiritually corrosive. Moving down the ladder is a slide away from what is virtuous toward what is destructive. The enemy aims to move people down that ladder one step at a time.

This chapter is not just about humor. It is about what humor reveals about the heart. The patient's social circle expands to include friends whose chief mode of interaction is scoffing, mocking, sneering, and treating all things as contemptible. These are not deep thinkers, noble leaders, or great tempters. They are clever enough to be dangerous, but their cleverness is wasted on tearing down rather than building up. Scripture warns that "scoffers set a city aflame" (Proverbs 29:8) and that in the last days "scoffers will come… following their own ungodly passions" (Jude 1:18). The scoffer's spirit resists truth, despises wisdom, and delights in cynicism. In our time, their numbers are growing.

"The Spirit is the indwelling wellspring of joy in God that we experience as we live by faith in the Son of God." -Galatians 2:20

Joy: The Deepest Longing

Joy is the hardest for the enemy to corrupt because joy is what we were made for. It's the deepest satisfaction of the human soul, a transcendent gift that flows from relationship with the living God. Joy isn't happiness, which depends on circumstances. Joy is something far deeper, rooted in the eternal rather than the temporary.

True joy always stems from the Lord, from relationship with Him. It springs from shared love, mutual affection, and the experience of God's presence in our lives. The demonic cannot fully understand it, much like they cannot comprehend the beauty of music in heaven. When scoffing shows up, joy is often the first casualty because cynicism cannot coexist with genuine delight in God and others.

Joy manifests in your countenance. You can see it in someone's face, hear it in their voice. It's relational, clean, and strengthening. And here's what makes joy so remarkable, it transcends difficult circumstances. You can experience profound joy even in the midst of trials because joy isn't tied to your external situation; it's tied to your relationship with God.

This is especially clear in worship. When you sing praise to God and engage with worship music, something happens. Joy feels like a two-way relationship, you sing to God, and the Holy Spirit comes over you. It can be intentionally activated, like a "joy switch," and it serves as a potent antidote to anxiety. I've experienced this kind of extreme joy in my relationship with Jesus Christ, and not just when everything is perfect in my life. True joy emerges from spiritual connection with the One who created you for Himself.

Joy creates bonds that deepen over time. It binds people together in a way cynicism cannot. It's a form of spiritual strength and a weapon against despair. The demonic hate it because they can never create it, only try to destroy it.

Fun and the Joke Proper

Fun refers to the play instinct and good-natured recreation. It refreshes the soul and strengthens relationships. The Joke Proper is harmless irony or wit that exposes life's incongruities. Both are gifts when used rightly, but both can become doors to something darker.

Fun is healthy when balanced with work and responsibility. Couples who have fun together and families that have fun together find more happiness than those who don't. But fun becomes unhealthy when pursued to excess or when it distracts from what matters most. God wants us to have fun and enjoy the world he made but not allow fun to become an idol.

Sometimes I feel churches lose sight of the importance and blessing of fun. These austere religious groups have a perspective that laughter is undignified, humor isn't holy, and fun is a distraction. I, for one, would want no part of a church like that. God owns all emotions, including humor, fun, and recreation. Children also love to have fun, and they should! My church has a motto that has become one of the pillars of their vision and ministry philosophy, "kids should drag their parents to church." Too often church becomes a place that is boring and uninviting to children. But Jesus said in Mark 10:14, "Let the little ones come to me." Remembering to keep fun and laughter in their good and proper place can help create a church that truly mirrors the culture of heaven.

The Joke Proper can be wholesome wit, but it can also slide into the crude, the sexual, or the demeaning. And here's where discernment is needed, what if your idea of fun is making fun of people less fortunate than you? We're all guilty of saying regrettable things to get a laugh, only to realize later it was demeaning to another person. People's struggles with weight, health, and beauty should not be fertile ground for our amusement. Even if you're alone, resist the temptation to find fun in other people's suffering.

Scripture warns against "filthiness nor foolish talk nor crude joking, which are out of place" (Ephesians 5:4). When jokes are used to degrade, they begin to take on the nature of scoffing. Making fun at someone's expense may get a laugh, but it trains the heart toward mockery rather than love.

All funny jokes have a semblance of truth built into them. But there's a line where the irony becomes more harmful than harmless. When you call someone out for this behavior, people will say it's harmless fun and that you're overthinking it. But you know it's destroying what should be your Christ-like mindset. This is where Fun and the Joke Proper begin their slide toward Flippancy.

Flippancy: The Scoffer's Native Tongue

Now we come to flippancy, the most dangerous form of laughter and the focus of our warning. This is where the real spiritual battle lies.

Flippancy dismisses serious matters with a smirk, treats truth as optional, and avoids responsibility by reducing everything to a joke. C.

S. Lewis identifies this as the scoffer's native tongue. It's defined as a lack of respect or seriousness, but it goes deeper than that. Flippancy is cynicism personified. Godly humor comes from a place of love and joy; Satan's humor comes from a place of criticism and mockery.

Scripture has much to say about this posture. Proverbs warn repeatedly about the mocker, "A scoffer does not like to be reproved; he will not go to the wise" (Proverbs 15:12). "The proud, haughty man, 'Scoffer' is his name; he acts with arrogant pride" (Proverbs 21:24). The scoffer is grouped with the wicked and sinners as someone to avoid, "Blessed is the man who walks not in the counsel of the wicked, nor stands in the way of sinners, nor sits in the seat of scoffers" (Psalm 1:1). Peter echoes this in the New Testament, "Scoffers will come in the last days with scoffing, following their own sinful desires" (2 Peter 3:3).

Flippancy also deadens intellect, kills affection, and fosters shallow, co-dependent bonds. Think of the social media user who responds to every serious news story with a sarcastic meme. The coworker who can't have a genuine conversation without turning it into mockery. The friend group where everyone competes to see who can be most cynical about relationships. These aren't isolated jokes; it's a posture that is taken on by these people toward life. Late-night comedy, viral memes, endless ridicule, sadly, our culture celebrates this kind of mockery. It's become all too common.

The Downward Pull of Flippancy

This is where we see the hierarchy in action, the gravitational pull downward from joy all the way to flippancy. The demonic cannot create joy, so they pull people down the ladder step by step until they reach the basement: cynicism and scoffing.

Flippancy requires little effort to maintain. Once a person is conditioned to respond with mockery, no further argument is needed. Their heart and mind disengage. They stop seeking truth and avoid situations that might demand genuine thought or sacrifice. The scoffer's life is easier than the builder's. It takes no courage to mock and no sacrifice to criticize. It's simpler to sit in the bleachers, jeering at those on the field, than to enter the game. Think of the "non-player character" from video games, background characters who exist to fill the scenery but aren't truly engaged in the action. In life, scoffers can become like them. They're present but not participating in building or contributing anything of value. Instead, they repeat the same lines of sarcasm, tribal talking points, and prepackaged outrage.

This pattern of constantly going for the lowest common denominator humor, typically crude and scoffing in nature, creates mental pathways that become harder and harder to break. We've talked before about trails in the woods, the more a path is walked, the more it becomes the familiar route. Flippancy works the same way. The more we mock, the more natural it becomes to respond with mockery in every situation. Over time, scoffing kills affection, deepens isolation, and leaves the heart cold.

Reclaiming Humor for the Kingdom

God created humor, and we can climb back up the ladder. Gravity pulls everything down, but with Christ, we move upward, we choose joy, and we redeem humor for the Kingdom of God.

The Bible is clear, "Blessed is the man who walks not in the counsel of the wicked, nor stands in the way of sinners, nor sits in the seat of scoffers" (Psalm 1:1). This isn't about pride or thinking you're better than anyone. It's about recognizing that who you laugh with shapes who you become. The more closely we bond with scoffers, the easier it is to adopt their posture.

The difference between godly humor and flippancy lies in the source. When we identify it as irony or laughter, it should flow out without malice rather than flowing out of criticism. One builds up, the other tears down. Good-natured humor in a godly community confounds the demonic because it strengthens affection, lightens burdens, and fosters unity.

As Reg notes from the film, *The Life of Brian*, "All right, but apart from the sanitation, the medicine, education, wine, public order, irrigation, roads, the fresh water system, and public health… what have the Romans ever done for us?"

The goal is not to become humorless, but to be intentional. Humor should never become a license for cruelty. When our laughter dishonors God's image in others, it damages our witness and hardens our hearts.

Reclaiming humor means:

- **Cultivating joy** that flows from worship and relationship with God, the kind the enemy cannot counterfeit.
- **Enjoying fun** that refreshes rather than distracts, that builds community and creates lasting memories.
- **Telling jokes** that enlighten rather than demean, that have wit without cruelty, that flow without criticism.
- **Rejecting flippancy's cheap shortcuts** by refusing to take the easy path of mockery and choosing the harder path of building up.

Your character is tested by what you find funny and how you engage with humor.

Practical Guardrails

- **Choose your company wisely.** The more time you spend with scoffers, the more your tone becomes yours. This isn't about being judgmental; it's about recognizing the power of influence.
- **Evaluate your default reaction.** When serious matters come up, do you instinctively mock, or do you listen first? Pay attention to your reflexes. Are you reaching for criticism or for understanding?
- **Ask the "love question."** Before you laugh, before you share that meme, before you make that comment, ask: Does this reflect love for God and neighbor? Does it build up or tear down?
- **Redeem your fun.** Intentionally plan activities that build memories, deepen relationships, and strengthen character. Make fun something that brings you closer to people, not something that creates distance through mockery.

Takeaway

The spirit of the scoffer is a uniquely destructive force in relationships, community, and the soul. It disengages heart and mind while pretending to be wise. It trades the hard work of building for the lazy thrill of tearing down. Scripture warns that scoffers will multiply in the last days, and our times confirm this.

But we can reclaim humor as a gift from God. We can resist the gravitational pull downward and climb back up the ladder toward joy. Root your humor in pure observation, enrich life with wholesome fun, sharpen laughter with wit that comes from delight, and protect joy from the corrosion of flippancy. In doing so, you guard your heart and bear witness to a Kingdom where laughter heals rather than harms.

A Closing Prayer

Heavenly Father, thank You for the gift of laughter and the deeper gift of joy. Thank You for creating me for relationship with You, where I can experience true joy even in difficult circumstances. Help me to guard my heart against the easy temptation of mockery and cynicism. Give me wisdom to know when humor builds up and when it tears down. Forgive me for the times I've chosen criticism over compassion, for the times I've used humor as a weapon rather than a gift. Shape my heart to be more like Christ, even in the way I laugh. Lord, hear my prayers and continue Your work in me. Amen.

Chapter 12
The Safest Road to Hell is the Gradual One

In Chapter 12, we explore how the slow fade works, how it leaves us lukewarm and spiritually ineffective, how it has unfolded across generations and nations, and how to resist it with a life of intentionality and action. C. S. Lewis reveals a dreadfully simple reality when he observed that "the safest road to hell is the gradual one. The gentle slope, soft underfoot, without sudden turnings, without milestones, without signposts." That single line captures a truth as old as Scripture and as relevant as the present moment.

Most people do not fall away from faith through one dramatic plunge into evil. It is far more common for a man or woman to slowly, almost imperceptibly, drift into spiritual ruin. The gradual slope is rarely obvious, and that is why it is so effective.

Scripture

"Therefore we must pay much closer attention to what we have heard, lest we drift away from it." - Hebrews 2:1

The Slow Fade

These letters reveal a profound narrative of subtle temptation and human vulnerability. Not every demonic tactic looks like a tabloid headline. Sometimes the Enemy aims for obvious, overt sins like lust, adultery, drunkenness, or fraud. Yet rather than overt vices, we often find ourselves fighting subtle tactics that seldom announce themselves as "sin." They do not shove you off the cliff. They nudge you toward a gentle slope.

Call it the slow fade. The demonic strategy is a methodical process of pulling an individual away from genuine connection with God, a little bit at a time. You do not wake up one morning and renounce Christ. You drift. One little concession here, one small delay there, one more day of "I will pray tomorrow," until you look up and realize your heart is cold and your zeal is gone.

Here is the twist, the slow fade often travels through empty things, not evil things. Not a plunge into scandal, but a thousand small diversions, endless scrolling, idle chatter, busy work that fills every margin, hobbies that soak up your best hours, chores that expand to the shape of your life. You are not bowing to Baal. You are just wasting time. And that is the point. A wasted life is victory enough for Hell.

Lewis's framing here echoes, and almost certainly draws on the Book of Common Prayer lectionary line, "O God… without whom nothing is strong, nothing is holy." He flips it brilliantly, without God, even "nothing" becomes strong. In seasons of spiritual coldness, the tiniest distractions, the kinds of things that would not have tempted you when you were close to the Lord, suddenly feel heavy enough to tie you down. That is the slow fade at work, "nothing" becomes strong.

This same tactic does not just happen to individuals. It happens to peoples. Think about the cultural changes that took place by inches, prayer in schools removed, the Ten Commandments taken out of public buildings, public life carefully quarantined from public faith. The separation of church and state slowly morphed from protecting the church from state control into a practical exclusion of faith from the public square. The changes were gradual, almost imperceptible year by year, but their cumulative effect is obvious now. A generation later, we look back and ask, when did we drift this far? That is the point. The same slow fade that hollows out a soul can hollow out a culture.

The lesson is not nostalgia. It is vigilance. Drift is normal when we are not intentional. The enemy is happy to let life feel "fine" while meaning, purpose, and calling quietly bleed out of the day.

Becoming Lukewarm in Life

The slow fade does not usually turn a Christian into a militant atheist. It turns a Christian into a lukewarm and ineffective believer. The goal is to transform a passionate believer into a disengaged one. We see this in several very practical areas in life. Parts of life that we fail to invest in slowly deteriorate.

Lukewarmness is dangerous precisely because it feels fine. You are in church. The bills are paid. You have not blown up your marriage, and your job's going well. You can point to a few good things, maybe you even serve once in a while. But inside, there is that dim uneasiness you would rather not face. And the Enemy is content to let you keep up appearances, because the externals prevent you from asking what is really going on inside. This not only affects your spiritual life. It starts to show up everywhere.

In marriage, you may tell yourself, "We are not fighting, we must be fine," yet the date nights disappear, careful conversations go missing, and long-term dreams never surface. Since Adam and Eve, the devil has been working to destroy the marriage union that God created. We tend to fall in love quickly, but when we fall back on our heels, we can fall out of love slowly. We need to be active and engaged to know what to work on to stay strong. It could have to do with sex, in-laws, or money issues, the three main reasons given in studies for the breakdowns in marriages. Issues like these and others never get addressed with a lukewarm mentality.

In parenting, you may think, "The kids kiss us goodnight, we must be doing okay," while intentional discipleship is crowded out by activities, screens, and hurry. At work, you reassure yourself, "I am still employed," even as excellence gives way to coasting, craft becomes a checkbox and calling turns into clock-punching. In health, you tell yourself, "I am tired, but who isn't?" while the exercise stops, the diet slides, the doctor visit is deferred, and a year later, you are a different person. We tell ourselves everything is fine, while the little neglects add up, the unfiled taxes, the oil change put off again, the room that never gets organized, the budget you will fix next month. In all these ways, we are withdrawing from accounts we stopped depositing in. And the sum of those withdrawals is a shattered life. That is how the slow fade works.

Here is the subtlety, sometimes the demonic does not tempt you to do bad things. It tempts you to do nothing. The plan is idleness dressed up as being "too busy," passivity disguised as "I will get to it," spiritual neglect disguised as "I am still in church." The result, as Screwtape describes it, is the patient doing "neither what I ought nor what I liked." Not the good I am called to, nor the good I even want. Just nothing. And because nothing can be strong when God is far away, the tiniest obstacles become ropes that bind. A nagging email you will not open, a phone call you avoid, a calendar block you refuse to make, a ten-minute prayer time that always gets bumped. In closeness with God, those things feel like pebbles. In drift, they feel like boulders.

This is why staying at the level of appearances is so deadly. You can be a faithful churchgoer and be spiritually frozen. You can have a stable marriage and be emotionally absent. You can have good kids and never disciple them. Externals can mask decay. The slow fade loves that mask.

How to Fight It: Rekindling Spiritual Engagement

You do not drift out of a rut. You act out of it. The cure starts with naming what is true, "I am drifting. I am lukewarm. I am wasting time." That honesty announces you are already in the spiritual battle. Now act. Not perfectly. Not theatrically. Just act.

Theodore Roosevelt once said, "Get action. Do things. Be sane. Do not fritter away your time. Create, act, take a place wherever you are, and be somebody. Get action!" That call to action is exactly what cuts against the slow fade. The battle is not won with grand gestures or dramatic vows, but with deliberate, consistent motion. Get action in prayer. Get action in Scripture. Get action in your marriage, with your children, with your neighbors, and in your church. Do not fritter away your time. Move forward, however small the step.

Here are a few practical ways to fight back against drift, the slow fade.

The Rule of Four

Reading the Bible is one of the most transformational habits a Christian can form. Yet studies consistently show that occasional or sporadic reading does not create lasting change. One day here or there brings encouragement, but it rarely shapes life. Two days a week still have little measurable effect. Even three days show only a marginal difference. But the research reveals a turning point, when Scripture is opened at least four days a week, lives change. Patterns shift. Desires are reoriented. Faith takes root in daily experience instead of sitting on the margins.

This is the threshold where God's Word starts shaping the majority of your week instead of the minority. That tipping point matters. It is not about legalism or hitting a quota, but about consistency that reorders your inner world. Make it simple and sustainable: one chapter, one psalm, one prayer, four days minimum.

The Power of 15 Minutes

The first 15 minutes are almost always the hardest part of any meaningful task. Whether you are drifting spiritually, stuck in a rut, facing something intimidating, or simply unmotivated to get started, that opening stretch feels like a wall. But once you begin, the wall often dissolves. A shift happens in the atmosphere. What seemed overwhelming suddenly becomes manageable.

This is the secret of the power of 15 minutes. Give yourself permission not to conquer the whole thing, but to start. Set a timer and push through the first quarter of an hour. More often than not, momentum will carry you forward well past the timer. And even if you stop, you have already gained ground.

Re-engage the Basics

Pray more, go to church with your family, and be charitable, not just with your money but with your time and skills. Do not just attend, participate. Sing like it matters. Take notes. Serve someone. Invite a friend. Show up early, stay late. If you have been a holiday Christian or a part-time one, this is where the drift ends: consistent presence.

In your marriage, plan the date now. Not after this busy stretch. In parenting, set one simple discipleship habit that happens every week, whether reading a psalm at dinner, praying at bedtime, or a Sunday walk to talk about the sermon. At work, choose one corner of your craft to sharpen this month.

As you start taking action to fight the drift, remember that grace meets motion. God doesn't steer a parked car. This is not self-salvation. We are not earning our way back. God is not waiting at the finish line with folded arms. He runs to the prodigal who takes the first step home. The same Spirit who convicts you of drift will empower you to move. You will feel weak at first. That is normal. You are not called to be strong in yourself but to be strong in the Lord and in the power of His might.

Takeaway

Each of us faces the subtle yet dangerous process of drifting away from faith. It's important to recognize distractions, resist spiritual complacency, and fully integrate faith into daily life. Name the slow fade in your life. Reject the mask of "it's fine." Re-engage with God and with the people and callings He has entrusted to you. Open Scripture. Pray short and honest before you pray long. Starve the nothing that has been eating your life. Take action. When you do, you will find the dim uneasiness giving way to conviction, then to joy, then to strength. Your lamp will burn brightly again. And the gentle slope will become a path that leads you back into the warmth of His presence.

The devil's sharpest weapon here against believers is not scandal. It is subtraction, a slow, quiet drift into nothing. He is content for you to keep focus on the external things if it prevents you from facing the truth. He is content for a nation to keep religious words in its mouth if it quietly forgets God in its life. Without God, nothing is strong, and in that emptiness, even trivial things bind us. By actively pursuing joy, prayer, and community, Christians can guard against becoming "lukewarm" and ensure their spiritual journey remains strong and purposeful.

A Closing Prayer

Lord, I need You to draw me closer to You in obedience. Help me to abide in Your Word and walk in faith each and every day. Forgive me for times of being a Sunday Christian, present in worship one day, but distant from You the rest of the week. Teach me to meet You daily in prayer and quietness of heart. Activate me to repent of drifting and help me turn every aspect of my life back to you. Help me to make sure my life is always and fully centered on Jesus. Amen.

Chapter 13
Quiet Revival

In the previous chapter, we confronted the danger of the slow fade, the gradual drift that pulls us away from God without us even noticing. We learned how to fight it with intentional action. But what about the other side of the story? What happens when God interrupts that drift? How does He call us back?

C. S. Lewis shows us exactly how this happens. In Letter 13, Screwtape is dismayed to discover that the patient's slow drift has suddenly ended. The patient goes for a simple walk and finds peaceful solitude, clean pleasure, and grateful communion. Screwtape describes this as an "asphyxiating cloud" of God's presence pushing the demonic back, and the patient awakens to grace in what amounts to a second conversion. In the quiet stillness of an ordinary moment, something extraordinary can happen. God meets us not with condemnation, but with gentle mercy. Not through a burning bush or a voice from heaven, but through a sunrise, a walk, a moment of peace that unexpectedly opens our hearts. Renewal often arrives in the ordinary. It comes when we create space for God through simple, clean pleasures enjoyed without guilt or performance. It comes when we think independently, free from the crowd's pressure. And when it comes, we must act. This chapter explores how God meets us in these quiet mercies, what prepares our hearts to receive them, and why conviction must become action if renewal is going to last.

"But the Advocate, the Holy Spirit, whom the Father will send in my name, will teach you all things and will remind you of everything I have said to you." - John 14:26

When Repentance Rekindles Faith

There is a kind of repentance that belongs to everyday discipleship. We confess, we adjust, and we keep walking. But there are also larger course corrections after a season of decline. These are not the first conversions of a soul to Christ, but they can feel like second beginnings. That is why Christians have always prayed for revival, not only for churches or nations, but for their own hearts.

One old hymn says it best. It is a song about the need for continual revival throughout life:

"All glory and praise to the God of all grace

who has bought us and sought us and guided our ways.

Hallelujah thine the glory. Hallelujah amen.

Hallelujah thine the glory. Revive us again."

That captures what we mean here. Renewal is grace. God interrupts our drift, not to shame us, but to give us another chance. Seasons rise and fall. Energy wanes and returns. That is normal. The danger is not the low place itself but staying there. Renewal is God's gift of clarity, and it comes with the desire to act. That desire is part of grace. It is wise to move quickly while the desire is fresh.

Sacred Pathways in Simple Joys

Renewal does not always come through dramatic events; not everybody will have a 'road to Damascus' moment. Often it arrives in the ordinary, on a walk, in the quiet of a chair, in a moment of enjoyment received without guilt or performance. Reading a book because it is good, not because it makes us look clever. Watching the sunrise, I am grateful simply to be alive. Drinking a hot cup of tea without distraction. A conversion can be remarkable in its simplicity. These are not "holy" moments in themselves, but when received in honesty and gratitude, they create space for God. It can be in the midst of everyday life or in a moment of unexpected joy that we can rediscover faith.

That is why even simple pleasures can become spiritually protective. They are not virtuous by category, but there is an innocence in them when they are received with gratitude. Self-forgetfulness pushes vanity aside. Pride has nothing to feed on. Envy finds little oxygen. Gratitude begins to rise.

Former Pastor of Westminster Chapel and renowned author, R. T. Kendall once described the Holy Spirit as sensitive as a dove. A dove will not land where there are agitation and harshness. It rests where there is peace. That picture helps us understand what happens when life grows simple and uncluttered. There are times when God's presence feels unusually near, what Lewis once pictured as an "asphyxiating cloud," overwhelming to the demonic and unexplainable to us. We cannot manufacture that, but we can prepare for it. Solitude instead of isolation. Gratitude instead of cynicism. Clean pleasures instead of numbing ones. These create an environment where the Spirit settles and stays.

Not everything we do in life is holy in God's eyes; things like watching TV, cooking food, or playing golf are neither good nor bad in essence. But God is the creator of all things good.

Is God a Fan of Golf?

If you are ever alone on a golf course in the countryside, the quiet and the majesty are truly breathtaking, and it is a great moment to find solitude and talk to your Father. Every time I find myself in these moments, I feel so truly blessed.

I remember one particular morning in the height of summer when I had stayed back in Arizona, where my family and I live, while they had gone to the beach in California. I booked the earliest tee time at a course out in the desert that only had one home on it and a trailer for a clubhouse. I woke at 4 AM and headed out to the course. I was the first to arrive; I beat all the workers and grounds crew. I took my clubs and headed to the chipping area; the quiet and balmy Arizona morning was amazing, and watching the sun come up before you play is a wonderful moment. I had been there for quite a while, and still, no one. Suddenly, I heard a buggy heading my way, and a grounds crew member asked me what I was doing there. I told him I had the first tee time, and they said, "Well, you need to check the date; we are closed today." My tee time was for the next day.

Seeing that I looked dejected, they asked if I wanted to walk the course as long as I had water. It ended up being one of the most memorable experiences of my life. I don't even remember my score that day, but I do remember the thunderous quiet, the magnificent views, and the wildlife roaming the course unabashed. I remember being nearly brought to tears by the breathtaking majesty. For me, the question "Does God play golf?" was answered. I would say He does, and He is a lot better than I am.

Moments like that are not holy because of golf itself. They are holy because God often meets people in gratitude and peace. Pure pleasures open doors. False pleasures close them. That is the contrast we must learn.

Reclaiming the God-Given You

There is another remarkable benefit to enjoying quiet moments with the Lord. When someone enjoys a thing for its own sake, without needing applause, they are harder to control. The person who can say, "I enjoy this because it is good," and does not care what others think is already shielded from many subtle pressures.

Even trivial tastes, a love of hot chocolate, stamp collecting, gardening, cricket, baseball, or hiking, can carry an innocence that lowers the volume of pride. They do not make us more virtuous, but they leave less room for envy and posturing. That is why independent thought is a real threat to the demonic. The demonic trembles at people who can think for themselves.

But independence is not just about resisting external pressure. It is also about receiving what God has put inside you. He made you with particular inclinations, preferences, and tastes, and He wants you to enjoy them without guilt. The sunset He painted, the game He let you love, the hobby that brings you peace, these are not distractions from Him. They are gifts from Him.

Here is where the wires often get crossed. God calls us to deny ourselves, but not by rejecting every innocent taste He has given. He asks us to deny selfishness and sin so that He can restore us to our true selves. The enemy inverts this. He urges us to indulge what should be crucified and to deny what should be received with gratitude. The result is confusion and shame. God untangles the wires by redeeming personality, refining tastes, and restoring what reflects His image.

Parents see this in miniature. One child's energy needs calming. Another's energy needs encouraging. The same outward behavior can spring from very different hearts. Good parenting corrects what is crooked and cultivates what is good. God does the same at full scale. He is not erasing uniqueness. He is redeeming it.

When God Speaks, Act

Renewal comes as a gift, but it requires a response. A change of heart without a change of action is a change of nothing.

Think of New Year's resolutions. They often begin with a sincere spark, this will be the year to get fit, to change habits, to start fresh. The first week is easy. Then life crowds in. The spark sputters. By February, the plan is gone. Do that two or three years in a row, and the spark itself weakens. You stop believing the feeling will last. The same pattern can happen spiritually. God meets you in a quiet moment, on a walk, in worship, sitting alone with Scripture. You feel His nearness. Conviction comes. You sense the nudge to change, to act, to make things right. But if you wait too long, the feeling fades. And the more often you feel conviction without acting on it, the harder it becomes to act at all. Eventually, you stop feeling it altogether.

The story of Pharaoh in Exodus is a sobering warning. In the early plagues, Pharaoh hardened his own heart. Each time he felt conviction, he resisted. He refused to act. Then the language shifts, God hardened Pharaoh's heart. That is not God turning soft clay into stone for no reason. It is God confirming what Pharaoh chose repeatedly. Refusal trains the heart to resist. Eventually, the resistance becomes permanent.

That is why windows of grace matter so much. When God convicts you in those still, quiet moments, when He meets you in renewal, do not delay. Do not assume the feeling will return tomorrow. Conviction is an invitation, and invitations have expiration dates.

So, what does action look like? It might mean making an apology you have been avoiding. Changing a bad habit that has been slowly poisoning your life. Opening your Bible again after months of neglect. Reassessing friendships that pull you away from Christ. Adjusting the way you speak, the places you go, the things you allow into your home. It might mean being willing to talk about God openly, to pray with your spouse, to disciple your children with intention.

If God is speaking directly about something in your life, you'll know what it is in your heart. The real journey begins when you are willing to transform your life, step by step and moment by moment. God meets you in grace. Your job is to meet Him in obedience. When conviction comes, move.

Takeaway

God often calls us back through quiet mercies. He interrupts drift and meets us in ordinary joys. He has not forgotten you. Even in the drift, even in the coldness, He is already at work preparing moments of grace to call you home. He meets you in the ordinary, in a quiet morning, in a simple pleasure enjoyed for its own sake, in the peace that settles when life grows uncluttered. These are not accidents. They are invitations.

When renewal comes, receive it with gratitude. Let the quiet moments speak. Enjoy the good gifts He has given you, the sunset, the walk, the game you love, without guilt or performance. Be yourself, the person He made you to be, free from the pressure to perform for the crowd. And when conviction stirs, when you feel that gentle nudge to change, to act, to make things right, do not delay. Move while the desire is fresh. A change of heart without a change of action is a change of nothing. But when you meet God's grace with obedience, repentance and renewal take root. So be intentional, find time to be in solitude and talk to the Father; what may seem like an ordinary moment can be transformed by the presence of the Lord.

A Closing Prayer

Lord Jesus, thank You for the calm, the peace, and the quiet solitude You provide. Thank you for allowing us to enjoy simple pleasures and for meeting us in the quiet and still moments of life. Help me to know when You are speaking. And give me strength and discipline to act in obedience. Thank you for being forgiving and long-suffering. Lead me and those around me to repentance, renewal, and revival. Lord, we love you! Amen.

Chapter 14
Humility and Pride

In Letter 14, Screwtape laments the patient now shows genuine humility as he recognizes that grace and gifts ultimately come from God and not himself. Frustrated, Screwtape schemes to corrupt this humility by tempting the patient to take pride in his "humble" state, subtly twisting gratitude for God's grace into self-congratulation, transforming a God-centered virtue into a self-centered trap, pride!

Pride and Humility are two of the most defining forces in the Christian life. We all know people who fall into these two camps. Pride blinds us to reality, inflates our self-importance, and ultimately isolates us from both God and others. Humility grounds us in truth, steadies us through life's ups and downs, and draws us closer to the grace of God. There is a balance between humility and pride; true humility is not about belittling oneself but recognizing and using God-given talents appropriately. Lewis Life's ups and downs become less extreme as one grows in faith, leading to more stability and consistent humility. And yet humility, when rightly understood, is not weakness or self-deprecation, but a confident steadiness rooted in God's gifts and grace.

Scripture

"But He gives more grace. Therefore, He says, "God resists the proud, But gives grace to the humble." Therefore, submit to God. Resist the devil and he will flee from you." - James 4:6-10

The Nature of True Humility

Humility is not about belittling yourself. It is not pretending you are worthless, talentless, or insignificant. True humility is the steady recognition that every good gift and every grace flows from God, and that we are utterly dependent on Him.

In the early days of faith, zeal often carries a kind of youthful boastfulness: bold promises of endless virtue, confidence that failure will never come, dreams of being a missionary or a hero for God. But as life unfolds, we encounter sin, dry seasons, and failure. We fall, we drift, and then by God's mercy we are drawn back. That process tempers us. It reshapes confidence into humility because we know we cannot stand on our own strength. We recognize daily dependence on grace.

Humility is truth. It is neither thinking too highly of ourselves nor too lowly. As has often been said, humility is not thinking less of yourself; it is thinking of yourself less. It is aligning our judgment of ourselves with God's truth.

Micah 6:8 captures this beautifully, "He has shown you, O mortal, what is good. And what does the Lord require of you? To act justly, to love mercy, and to walk humbly with your God." Walking humbly means living in reality, acknowledging our weakness, our dependence, our sin, and God's abundant grace.

Even how we handle praise is a window into humility. When someone offers us a gift or a compliment, false modesty may brush it aside with, "Oh no, it was nothing." Pride may puff up and say, "Yes, I worked hard, I deserve this." True humility receives with gratitude. It recognizes the gift as something from God and something to steward. Ironically, it takes humility to receive. To accept a blessing acknowledges dependence, acknowledges relationship, and keeps us grounded in truth.

The Subtlety of Pride

Pride is obvious in some places. Hollywood elites bask in the worship of adoring fans. Musicians stand on stage, flooded with applause, and may come to believe they are gods in their own right. Actors live under the flash of cameras, worshiped for beauty or fame. Even pastors are not immune, superstar leaders who become the main attraction for their congregations find themselves on dangerous ground. These are the loud, overt forms of pride, easy to spot from the outside.

But pride can be more subtle, and it seeps into every heart. It shows up in the constant need for affirmation, in insecurity that craves attention, and in exaggerating success to mask hidden weakness. Some pride is loud and pompous, but much of it is quiet and desperate, the broken heart trying to cover its emptiness by demanding recognition.

Pride often hides in the shadows of our daily work and passions. The butcher, baker, or candlestick maker may take quiet satisfaction in their craft, but pride can creep in when they begin to see their skills as self-made, forgetting the divine source of their abilities. The Gospels note the professions of Jesus' disciples, such as fishermen, a tax collector, and a carpenter, not to elevate their work but to show how ordinary lives can reflect God's purpose. Subtle pride emerges when we view our talents or roles as measures of our worth, rather than as gifts meant to serve others and glorify God.

This quiet pride can also twist our view of others' successes. It's natural to feel joy when our children excel, but pride subtly shifts the focus when we start to see their achievements as extensions of our own value. A child's good grades or hard work might spark a parent's boast, not just in the child's effort but in their own parenting prowess. This is where pride becomes insidious, turning even love into a platform for self-elevation, masking itself as care or celebration.

Humility, by contrast, anchors us against these subtle tides of pride. It calls us to recognize that every talent, every success, whether ours or our children's, is a gift from God, not a personal trophy. Humility doesn't diminish our joy in accomplishments; it redirects it, allowing us to celebrate without claiming the spotlight. A humble heart gives thanks for the blessing, honors the effort, and resists the urge to make someone else's victory a reflection of our own glory.

The subtlety of pride lies in its ability to disguise itself as virtue, love, ambition, or even gratitude. Whether in the quiet satisfaction of a job well done or the pride we take in our children, it whispers that we are the source of our own success. Humility counters this by pointing us back to God, reminding us that every good thing comes from Him. Only by staying vigilant and grounded in gratitude can we keep pride's subtle influence at bay.

Counterfeit Humility

If pride fails, the demonic has a counterfeit, false humility. C. S. Lewis notes that demons tempt people into believing humility means a pretty woman trying to think herself ugly or a clever man trying to convince himself he is a fool. But that is not humility at all. That is dishonesty, and dishonesty never honors God.

False humility blinds us to truth. It teaches us to deny God's gifts, rather than receive them with gratitude. It is, in its own way, just another form of pride, because it is still obsessed with the self. It obsesses over appearing humble rather than actually walking in truth.

The devil loves to cross the wires here. Where God tells us to repent of sin, Satan tells us to embrace it as "who we are." Where God tells us to embrace His gifts, Satan tells us to deny them. He urges us to reject the very things God gave us for blessing others, while clinging to the sinful things that destroy us.

True humility accepts the gifts God has given, not as grounds for boasting, but as opportunities for stewardship. It says, "Yes, God has made me skilled, beautiful, talented, or wise in this area, and my joy is to use it for Him and to bless others."

Living Examples of Humility

Sometimes the best way to see the difference between pride, false humility, and true humility is through simple, real-world examples.

When someone compliments you for something you do well in life, do you feel the adoration, or do you give credit to the God who blessed you with the opportunity and talent? Appreciating that God doles out talents to us is important to acknowledge. People can easily become depressed and feel worthless if they have not found what they are good at or called to do in life.

Consider the illustration of a cook. When praised, there are three possible responses:

- **Dismissal**: "Oh, it's not that special." This is false modesty. It denies the truth, diminishes the gift, and discourages others. It makes them feel that they cannot get close to the standard that they celebrate, yet that you diminish.
- **Arrogance**: "Yes, I worked hard, I'm just naturally good at this." This is vainglory. It makes the talent all about self and subtly elevates the cook above others. It makes others who work hard but can't reach your level now feel that other forces are holding them back from being as good as they too, put in a lot of hard work.
- **Gratitude**: "God has blessed me with this ability, and I try to honor Him by using it well." This is humility. It accepts the compliment truthfully while directing praise to God. You have humbled yourself, and God will lift you up. Others can do some soul-searching for the blessings that God has for them, and it encourages them to work harder to honor God.

This third response encourages others rather than diminishing them. It lifts their eyes to God as the giver of all gifts. And it models the freedom of a humble heart that neither craves praise nor rejects it but simply receives it in truth.

Takeaway

Life is full of highs and lows. Pride tempts us to ride the highs too high, boasting, promising more than we can deliver, and exalting ourselves above others. False humility tempts us to ride the lows too low, self-deprecation, despair, and denying the gifts God has given.

But humility steadies us. It keeps our eyes outward, fixed on God and others.

Think of running a race. The runner does not stop to ask, "Am I great? Am I terrible?" He just runs. So too in the Christian life, humility frees us from obsession with self, whether in pride or false modesty, and allows us to run our race faithfully.

Every day is a new opportunity to repent, to receive grace, and to walk humbly. We do not need endless promises of perpetual virtue. We need steady obedience, daily grace, and outward focus. Humility means forgiving quickly, repenting often, and living with attention turned away from self and toward God and neighbor.

A Closing Prayer

Lord God in Heaven, Forgive me, for I have sinned against You with boastful pride, thinking I am more important than I truly am. Thank You for the gifts and talents You have given me; I will use them to honor You all of my days. I am humbled before You, O Lord. Keep my eyes fixed on You and my heart filled with the Holy Spirit, that I may pour myself out in love for others. My God, I give You glory for all that I am. Amen.

Chapter 15
Breaking Anxiety's Grip

In the quiet of his study, C. S. Lewis leaned forward, his fingers tracing the delicate lines of the manuscript that explores one of humanity's most profound spiritual struggles. Anxiety, he understood, was not merely an emotion but a demonic strategy, a subtle weapon designed to tear humans away from the sacred present.

The demonic realm understands something crucial, when our minds are fixated on potential disasters or imagined triumphs, we miss the sacred reality of today. This letter exposes how anxiety functions as a spiritual weapon, pulling us away from where God actually meets us, right here, right now. Lewis points out that the demonic will always try to get us to go in one of two directions, either tortured fear or stupid confidence. This revelatory tactic, once identified and confronted with a biblical strategy, will change how anxiety affects your life exponentially.

Scripture

"Be anxious for nothing, but in everything by prayer and supplication, with thanksgiving, let your requests be made known to God; and the peace of God, which surpasses all understanding, will guard your hearts and minds through Christ Jesus." - Philippians 4:6-7

Anxiety's Grip

If there is a pandemic that afflicts society, it is the demonic virus of anxiety. When we come to terms with the idea that anxiety serves many purposes, and none of them are good, it makes one wonder, *is this a demonic super weapon?*

Anxiety can lock up the most resourceful, skilled, and dedicated people in our world. Leaders can suffer and not make wise decisions, great singers may experience stage fright, public speaking is certainly cursed with it, and new relationships are scuttled because of the anxiety or fear of *Will they say no,* or *What could happen, etc.* Anxiety is a brilliantly subtle tool that will hold you back from fulfilling your God-given potential, becoming a better person, and getting closer to God.

Can you be anxious and present? The answer is no. Anxiousness is the antithesis of the present; anxiety draws you into worrying about future events and happenings and imaginary scenarios built on fear.

Living in anxiety means you won't be present with your children, family, friends, or spouse. We have all experienced moments of being asked to put our phones down and be present with our loved ones. Anxiety is just another distraction that you need to put away to become present. God wants us to wisely plan for the future as He gives us our daily bread, a metaphor to live in the present, but anxiety separates you from a relationship with God, as you can't meet with the Lord for your daily bread when your mind is only fixed on the future.

The Enemy's Two-Pronged Strategy

Lewis observed something crucial, when anxiety strikes, the demonic realm tries to push us toward one of two extremes. In Screwtape's words, "Tortured fear and stupid confidence are both desirable states of mind." Either response accomplishes the enemy's goal.

"Tortured fear" is neurotic hyperactivity. It's the spinning mind that catastrophizes everything. Fear of losing your job, watching a relationship collapse, seeing your children make destructive choices, worrying about finances, health crises, or economic collapse. The stress compounds, cortisol floods your system, and you're paralyzed by scenarios that haven't happened and may never happen.

"Stupid confidence" sits at the opposite extreme. It's naive passivity, telling yourself everything will be fine simply because you can't handle facing reality. Sometimes it's pride, but often it's fear dressed up as confidence. It's saying "I'm sure it'll work out" not because you have a good reason to believe it will, but because you're scared, naive, or simply refusing to deal with what's actually happening. It's retreating from responsibility rather than facing the truth.

Here's the insight that changes everything, the demonic realm wins with either response. But here's what both extremes have in common, neither stops to ask, "Is this true?" With tortured fear, we don't ask whether our catastrophic scenarios are reasonable or our anxiety proportionate to reality. With stupid confidence, we don't ask whether our optimism is justified or grounded in truth. Both are forms of living in unreality, and when we're not walking in truth, we deceive ourselves, and the demonic wins.

Jesus said, He is the way, the truth, and the life. When your mind is grounded in truth, in facts, in actual reality, you find peace. You experience a calm, settled confidence that can face whatever comes. But when anxiety has you fixating on hypothetical futures or stupid confidence has you ignoring reality, you're not walking in truth. And when we're not walking in truth, we can't commune with God. We dwell with the enemy instead.

Where God Meets Us

Here's the profound truth at the heart of this chapter, the present moment is where eternity touches time. It's the one place where we, as time-bound humans, can truly commune with our eternal God.

God exists outside of time. He has already orchestrated the past and is already orchestrating the future. He is eternal. The past, present, and future are all the same to the Lord. But we are created beings living in time. We have memories of the past and anticipation of the future, but we can only actually live in the present moment. Right now. This breath. This heartbeat. This is where God meets you.

Think about it carefully, anxiety lives in the future. In any current, immediate moment, you are alive, you are fine. Any worry about death, any dread about what's coming, means your mind has left the present and is gazing toward the future with fear. The demonic realm exploits this. Satan wants to pull us out of the present, away from where God meets us, into obsession with the past or future.

The past can become a weapon when Satan uses it to accuse us, to drown us in shame over our failures and sins. The future becomes a weapon when he fills us with anxiety about things that haven't happened and may never happen. Both pull us away from communion with God.

Here's a warning worth remembering, when you spend excessive time dwelling on past regrets or future fears, be careful. You may be spending time with Satan rather than God.

Now, does this mean we ignore the past and future entirely? Absolutely not. That would be foolish. God wants us to have a healthy relationship with both, but that relationship happens in the present, with His wisdom guiding us. We should think about the past to learn from it, to seek forgiveness where needed, to correct mistakes that still have consequences today. Likewise, we should think about the future to plan wisely, to be prudent, to provide for our families. But we do this in the present, with trust in God's provision, not consumed by fear or anxiety. THIS is the duty of today. This is what it means to be responsibly present.

Consider the Israelites in the wilderness. God gave them manna, bread from heaven, but only enough for one day. They were instructed not to save it for tomorrow. Why? Because gathering only what you need for today is an act of faith. It requires trusting that the Lord will provide tomorrow as well. "This is the day the Lord has made," Psalm 118:24 declares. Not yesterday. Not tomorrow. Today.

Here's a powerful illustration, if you found out you only had 30 days to live, what would you do? Here's a profound answer, "I would plant a tree." You won't live to see that tree grow. No one can guarantee it will survive. Developers might tear it down. Future owners might neglect it. But that shouldn't stop you from planting it. Be aware of the future, focus on the duty God has given you today, but don't worry about outcomes you can't control. Just plant the tree.

The present moment is where God gives us our daily bread and walks with us. When we meet with God in prayer about our future, we're having a conversation with our Father about our needs and desires. These conversations can reduce anxiety if we truly lay our troubles at His feet. Psalm 55:22 invites us, "Cast your burden on the Lord, and He shall sustain you; He shall never permit the righteous to be moved."

That's our journey as believers. We're called to trust God's grace for today and trust that He'll provide tomorrow's grace when tomorrow comes. When we live this way, we live in active communion with God.

Most people's biggest regret in life centers on the time they wasted rather than the memories they made and the love they shared with their family. When you live for today, walking with God in the present, you'll have far fewer regrets as you age. This is why we focus on today. This is why we don't let Satan pull our attention into anxious futures. God meets us here, now, and it's an act of faith to trust Him with tomorrow while we cherish, value, and live fully in the gift of today.

Planning vs. Worrying

As we live in the present, we still understand that tomorrow is going to come. So planning is important and can actually reduce anxiety. If we never consider the future, we're fools. Proverbs 22:3 says, "The prudent sees danger and hides himself, but the simple go on and suffer for it." The prudent person sees danger and makes adjustments. The simple person doesn't and pays for it. How will I raise my children? What about their education? How do I prepare for retirement? If I live where there are seasons, how do I prepare in summer for what's coming in winter?

There's a basic aspect of life that requires us to prepare for what's to come. Jesus rebuked crowds for knowing how to read the weather but not the spiritual signs of His coming. We need to be future-minded about natural patterns, business cycles, dry seasons and flowing seasons, knowing when to build barns and when to sow.

So, here's the key, planning is the duty of today. We're still living in the present, embracing the day the Lord has made and the duty He's called us to, while knowing tomorrow will come.

I believe in planning. I follow Dave Ramsey's approach to finances, planning for retirement, organizing estates, and carrying life insurance. But I'm not overwhelmed by fear of what may come. I'm planning to be prepared and protect my family in case of tragedy, but I'm not consumed by it. It's my duty today to be mindful and responsible for what may happen tomorrow, done with faith rather than fear.

Here's a principle worth memorizing, if you're focusing on the future and anything is stopping you from having calm, settled peace, consider whether that might be a demonic thought. If you're filled with fear, willing to compromise your values, or willing to skip doing the right thing to avoid a negative outcome or control a positive one, stop. Ask the Lord, "Is this a foothold of the enemy in my life, causing me to embrace tortured fear or stupid confidence about the future?"

Takeaway

The first step to conquering anxiety is acknowledging it as a weapon of the enemy. Then you must make yourself more present in the now. With family, put your phone down, turn off distractions, and engage face-to-face with your loved ones. At work, be diligent and ready to meet today's challenges while trusting God to bless or redirect your future plans.

When we refuse to be held captive by anxiety about the future, we reclaim our spiritual birthright, living fully in the here and now. Plant your tree. Receive your daily bread. Live in the sacred present where eternity touches time. Adopt a heart of gratitude for everything, even the smallest blessings. Praise and worship the Lord for every breath, every moment, and refuse to dwell on fears that would have you wallowing in anxiety. Take your troubles and lay them at His feet. You are forgiven. Christ has paid the price on the cross. Return to joy. This is the antidote. Do this and watch the demons flee.

A Closing Prayer

Dear Lord, let me not fall into the devil's trap of being anxious about things I cannot control or things that may never happen. Help me to cherish every moment of every day. Help me to never let my duty for today turn into fear about tomorrow. Protect me from my flesh and the Enemy, both of which cause me to spiral with anxiety. I cast my cares upon you, thank you for caring for me! Amen!

Chapter 16
The Sacred Assembly

In Letter 16, Screwtape probes deeper into why his patient has become so faithful to one particular church. This line of questioning reveals a critical truth; regular church attendance can be either a sign of spiritual vitality or spiritual stagnation. The very fact that we show up every Sunday tells us nothing about the condition of our hearts or the health of our faith. What matters is not just that we gather, but why we gather and how we engage with the body of Christ around us.

The role of the church has always been under demonic attack, and today we face unique challenges. We see the splintering of denominations over secondary issues, apostate churches that twist Scripture to fit cultural narratives, and believers who become either apathetic consumers or harsh critics of the very communities called to nurture their faith. To preserve the transformative power of spiritual community, we must learn to navigate these waters with both discernment and humility.

Scripture

"And they devoted themselves to the apostles' teaching and to fellowship, to the breaking of bread and to prayer." -Acts 2:42

The Right Reasons

Christian spirituality has no pause button. We are either growing closer to Christ or drifting away from Him. This reality makes our motivation for church attendance a crucial indicator of our spiritual health. Screwtape probes Wormwood to discover why the patient has become faithful to one particular church, and it's a question worth asking ourselves: Why do I go to church?

Some believers fall into what we might call "routine righteousness," attending faithfully but driven more by habit than hunger for God. They're there for the community, they're there because they feel good, they're there to check off their spiritual obligation without really investing in their faith. That does not lead to growth.

Others attend church from genuinely sincere hearts, eager to grow and learn, hungry for God's Word and fellowship with other believers. These are the ones who come with open hearts, ready to receive and contribute.

Still others come with wrong motivations entirely. Perhaps they come to feel superior, to judge others, to network for business, or simply because it makes them look respectable. The demonic realm loves to see believers attend church for the wrong reasons because it corrupts the very thing meant to strengthen them.

Many Christians also experience a common cycle, a season of spiritual failure followed by restoration. They walk away from faith, fall into sin, and then are graciously drawn back to the Lord. This experience fundamentally changes their approach to church attendance. Gone are the confident resolutions and lavish promises of perpetual virtue that often characterize new believers. Instead, they now come to church with a humble recognition of their need for daily grace.

This kind of humbled faith produces the healthiest church attendance. When we've experienced both spiritual victory and spiritual defeat, we develop what we might call "humble confidence." We no longer attend church, believing we have all the answers or that we're beyond the reach of temptation. Instead, we come as grateful recipients of grace, eager to receive what God wants to give us and ready to contribute to the growth of others. The Lord doesn't want us to be overly boisterous, promising to do more than we're able to do. He just wants faithfulness.

That's why it matters to find a church in your community, plant your family there, consider serving, attend regularly, not only when you feel the need. Beyond sound teaching, seek a church that offers true fellowship, mutual support, meaningful engagement, and a loving challenge to your own self-centeredness.

One Faith, Many Flavors

One of the most beautiful aspects of the church is its ability to unite people across lines that typically divide. The cross of Jesus Christ transcends denomination, demographic, cultural background, socioeconomic status, age, and culture.

As we established previously in our discussion of closed-handed and open-handed issues, there are core tenets we must hold firmly and secondary matters where faithful believers can disagree. We rally around the closed-handed issues like the authority of Scripture and the deity of Christ, while recognizing that open-handed matters like worship styles and church governance can vary among faithful congregations.

Throughout church history, denominations have formed around both doctrinal differences and practical considerations. Some churches emphasize liturgical worship with formal prayers and traditional hymns, while others embrace contemporary music and spontaneous expression. These differences reflect the beautiful complexity of the body of Christ. Different churches serve different purposes and minister effectively to different groups of people.

There are churches that do really well with ministering to new believers and casting the net to the lost. These churches often function almost like nurseries, where people enter the world of faith and receive the milk they need when they're young in their walk with Christ. On the other hand, there are churches that focus more on doctrine, really unpacking the nuance of theology, but those churches can make the barrier of entry too high for seekers and new believers.

The danger comes when we lose sight of what unifies us or when denominational pride replaces gospel humility. When we become cliquish, when we become arrogant about our particular stripe of Christianity, that's when the demonic realm ultimately wins. That's when our focus turns to being right about everything rather than letting Jesus be lifted up and worshiped.

Discernment vs. Criticism

Perhaps no temptation is more dangerous to churchgoers than the spirit of criticism. Screwtape specifically advises Wormwood to encourage the patient to become a connoisseur of churches. Someone who can walk into any congregation and immediately begin cataloging what's wrong with their doctrine, their music, their preaching, or their people.

The difference between healthy discernment and destructive criticism lies primarily in our heart attitude. It's actually a good thing to be at a church and not agree with everything. If you are at a church and agree with absolutely everything and love absolutely everything about the church, you probably are a little bit undiscerning and are just going along with the convenient thing. But the mark of a mature believer is someone who's able to say, "I can get on board with, submit to, and help advance the vision of the leadership of this church, even though I don't agree with every little thing." It's a heart that says, "I want to help be the solution to problems, not just a critic." The demonic wins when a believer takes the position of having haughty eyes that are looking down at people rather than having eyes that are bowed down to Jesus. Our gaze needs to be fixed, not downward at those around us, but upward in reverence and worship to the Lord.

We should be trying to understand each other rather than being a critic or a connoisseur. A critic is really somebody who tears people down, and the heart of the believer should be to build each other up. There should be a very healthy awareness of the strengths and weaknesses of different churches, but being aware of those varying strengths and weaknesses should come from a heart of unity and collaboration, and support for all of the churches that are really trying to lift up the name of Jesus.

It's very dangerous to have an overly strong or contentious opinion about the smaller areas of church doctrine and practice, but it's equally problematic not to care. So, it's a fine line that believers need to walk.

Drawing the Line

Now, here's the tension, we must guard against an overly critical spirit while also exercising genuine discernment. Some churches have not merely failed in methodology; they've abandoned biblical truth altogether. Lewis himself observed this danger. Screwtape describes a vicar who has "been so long engaged in watering down the faith… that it is now he who shocks his parishioners with his unbelief, not vice versa."

We say this with grief, not glee. These are not churches to mock but to mourn.

While we must guard against an overly critical spirit, we cannot ignore the reality that some churches and pastors have indeed wandered from biblical faithfulness. Some churches selectively choose outrage based on the pastor's political leanings without backing up their message with Scripture, distorting the faith, and creating their own word while misattributing it to God.

Modern Christianity faces significant challenges, including the tendency to water down biblical teachings to make them more palatable. Some pastors and churches compromise doctrinal integrity, adapting messages to cultural trends rather than maintaining the transformative power of the original scriptural teachings. Most of the time, they've gone woke because they've replaced their central pursuit of a gospel that transforms sinful and fallen mankind with pursuing a message of reforming social systems that they view to be flawed.

I attended a Catholic church in Scottsdale where the priest preached a sermon arguing for open borders without addressing the accompanying dangers, while giving a soft approach to pro-life issues. When I confronted him after Mass, he was militantly dismissive. His politics were clearly stronger than his faith. I must add that I have also been to other Catholic churches that, without hesitation, condemn abortion in the strongest terms. If any church cannot speak up ardently against abortion and the murder of the unborn and take a pro-life position, they are a wayward church. It's one thing to officially take a position on an issue, but without action, it is hollow and pointless.

When we encounter churches with compromised leadership, discernment requires us to respond appropriately. Be blunt with yourself, if the teaching has departed from biblical truth on closed-handed issues, leave. You're not likely to steer the ship back on course, and your time is better spent building up faithful churches with a clear Godly vision. This might mean having honest conversations with church leaders to gain clarity, but once you can see the compromise is real and entrenched, get out.

Takeaway

The church described in Acts 2:42 provides a timeless model, "They devoted themselves to the apostles' teaching and to fellowship, to the breaking of bread and to prayer." We gather around the preaching of the word because faith comes by hearing and hearing by the word of Christ. We focus on genuine fellowship, communion, and prayer.

Rather than approaching church as consumers, we should come as contributors eager to build up the body of Christ. Take the weekend message and carry it through your week. Get involved in small groups and meet people after church. Ask what the church is spending your generous gifts on. Volunteer to serve and be charitable with both your money and your time.

Remember that you are the church, not just someone who attends church. The building and programs are tools to facilitate what really matters, a community of believers gathering to worship God, grow in faith, and serve others. The church's strength lies not in perfection but in genuine commitment to spiritual community, unwavering dedication to the core message of the Christian faith and defending it boldly in the world today.

A Closing Prayer

Dear Lord, I pray for the faithful believers who gather to worship, fellowship, pray, and study Your Word. Pour out Your blessing upon all those who are seeking to be the church for the right reasons. Bring to light any wrong or misguided motivations in our hearts. Please strengthen church leadership, my pastor and all the pastors in this country who are trying to preach Your Word. Give them boldness, courage, strength, vision, and protect them from compromise and fear. We pray for revival in this country. For people to stand up for truth and to gather in Your name. In Jesus might name, Amen!

Chapter 17
The Sin of Gluttony

When we find ourselves consumed by small indulgences that gradually shape our character, we must ask, are these appetites serving God's purposes in our lives, or are they serving only ourselves?

In Screwtape Letter 17, Screwtape challenges Wormwood's fixation on traditional gluttony, the simple excess of eating too much food. Screwtape reveals a more subtle and perhaps more dangerous form, the gluttony of delicacy. This isn't about consuming massive quantities, but about developing insatiable, refined preferences that can never be met without intense labor from others. It's the difference between eating everything on the buffet and sending your meal back three times because it isn't prepared exactly to your specifications.

The relationship we have with even something as basic as food reveals profound truths about the disposition of our hearts and our capacity for self-control in every area of life.

Scripture

"For everything created by God is good, and nothing is to be rejected if it is received with thanksgiving, for it is made holy by the word of God and prayer." - 1 Timothy 4:4-5

The Gluttony of Delicacy

Most people understand gluttony as eating too much food, the classic image of excess that leads to obesity and health problems. This gluttony of excess is real and problematic, especially in our culture, where processed foods and instant gratification have created epidemic levels of poor health. When we don't take care of our physical bodies, it directly impacts our spiritual effectiveness.

But Screwtape points to something more insidious, the gluttony of delicacy. This isn't about quantity at all. It's about an excess of refinement, an excess of preference, an excess of priority placed on having fine things exactly our way. Lewis gives the example of a woman who sends her plate back to the waiter, saying, "No, no, that's far too much. Please send it back and bring me just a quarter of it." Her demanding attitude toward food is just as problematic as eating too much. It's the Downton Abbey level of pickiness, demanding that tea be served at precisely the right temperature with exactly the right type of biscuit and just the right proportion of jam.

Here's what makes this so dangerous, when our refined preferences become requirements, they transform into idols. God wants us to have good things. He created wine, fine foods, and countless pleasures for us to enjoy. But when we need them too often, when we prioritize them too highly, when we can't be satisfied without them, we've crossed a line. Our preferences have become masters rather than servants.

We all have this tendency in some aspects of our lives. Whether it's being particular about how our steak is cooked, insisting our coffee be prepared a certain way, or having very specific preferences about countless daily details, there's a fine line between appreciating quality and becoming enslaved to our preferences. The difference lies not in having preferences, but in what happens when those preferences aren't met. Do we graciously adapt, or does our day get ruined? Do we maintain perspective, or do we become demanding and difficult?

This gluttony of delicacy often reveals itself through a spirit of ingratitude. Instead of receiving what we're given with thanksgiving, we focus on what's wrong, what's missing, or how things could be better. It's the opposite of the contentment Scripture calls us to cultivate, and it can make us miserable even when surrounded by abundance.

Refining Creation as Worship

Here's where we must walk carefully because God actually calls us to refine the created order. The dominion mandate in Genesis commands us to "be fruitful and multiply and fill the earth and subdue it." This means taking the raw materials of creation and developing them into something more beautiful, more useful, more reflective of God's glory. The culinary arts are a perfect example of this calling, taking basic ingredients and, through skill, knowledge, and creativity, producing something that brings joy and nourishment.

When we study the science behind cooking the perfect steak, understanding different cuts of meat, how grass-fed versus grain-finished cattle produce different flavors, and the precise temperature needed to achieve the perfect sear, we're living out our purpose as image-bearers of God. This is humanity fulfilling its role as God's representatives, uncovering the hidden potentials He built into creation.

Proverbs 25:2 says, "It is the glory of God to conceal a matter, but the glory of kings is to search it out." When we discover better ways to prepare food, create beauty, or enhance experiences, we're participating in God's ongoing work in the world. Isaiah 25:6 describes the heavenly banquet with "the finest of wines and the choicest of meats." These aren't accidents; they represent the culmination of human skill applied to God's creation.

But here's where the tightrope appears, there's a difference between enjoying these refined experiences and worshiping them. When we eat at a friend's house and something isn't quite right, we graciously overlook it and focus on the relationship. But at a restaurant, we can become demanding, treating servers as if their worth depends on meeting our exact specifications.

This reveals the heart issue, are we using our refined tastes as tools of worship and gratitude, or have we turned them into idols that we expect others to serve? The same meal that could be received with joy and thanksgiving can become a source of pride, selfishness, and ingratitude depending on our heart posture.

Special Occasions, Not Daily Expectations

The key to navigating this balance lies in understanding the difference between sacred occasions and daily expectations. Jesus demonstrates this beautifully throughout the Gospels. Most meals we see Jesus sharing are simple: breaking bread with disciples, eating with sinners, feeding crowds with basic loaves and fish. He received whatever hospitality was offered without complaint or special demands.

Yet this same Jesus will one day sit at the head of the Marriage Supper of the Lamb, enjoying what will undoubtedly be the finest feast in history. He will be served as the King of Kings, and there will be nothing pretentious or inappropriate about receiving that honor. The difference is the occasion and the heart posture.

There's nothing wrong with taking your wife to a five-star restaurant for your anniversary and expecting excellent service and expertly prepared food. That's a sacred occasion, a celebration of God's gift of marriage, and an appropriate time to enjoy the finest expressions of culinary art. The problem comes when we expect that level of service and precision every single day, when we can't be satisfied with a simple meal graciously prepared.

Jesus washing His disciples' feet provides the perfect counterbalance to any tendency toward pride in our refined tastes. Here was the King of the universe, choosing to take the role of the lowest servant. When we develop sophisticated tastes, we must maintain this servant's heart, ready to lay aside our preferences for the sake of others.

The sin isn't in appreciating fine things. It's in expecting them constantly or using them as weapons of pride. There's a spirit that says, "I deserve the best, and if I don't get it, someone has failed me." This attitude transforms gifts from God into idols we worship, and it makes us miserable in the process. The solution is simple but profound, enjoy excellence when it's appropriate but be content with simplicity as your daily bread.

Mastering Our Appetites

Ultimately, the issue with both types of gluttony comes down to a fundamental spiritual principle, either we will master our appetites, or our appetites will master us. The same lack of self-control and gluttony of delicacy can manifest in sexual temptation, materialism, entertainment, or countless other areas.

Self-discipline is one of the most valuable virtues we can develop. It's not about becoming joyless or rigid, but about being free. When we master our desires instead of being mastered by them, we gain the freedom to enjoy God's gifts without being enslaved to them. We can appreciate fine things without needing them. We can adapt to simple circumstances without resentment. We become people who can be content in any situation.

Humility plays a crucial role here. The gluttony of delicacy often springs from pride and a sense of entitlement. We think we deserve the best, that our refined tastes make us superior, that others should labor to meet our standards. But humility recognizes that every good gift comes from God, not from our own merit. It receives what's offered with gratitude rather than demanding what we prefer.

Proverbs 23:1-2 warns us, "When you sit down to eat with a ruler, observe carefully what is before you, and put a knife to your throat if you are given to appetite." This isn't advocating self-harm, but emphasizing the critical importance of self-control, especially in situations where others are watching. The mark of spiritual maturity is being someone who has learned to regulate their tastes, desires, and appetites rather than being dominated by them.

This becomes crucial when we're in important situations, business dinners, social gatherings, or any context where our character is being observed. If we haven't learned self-control in the small, private moments of daily eating, we won't have it available when it matters most. Our private relationship with food reveals and shapes our capacity for self-discipline in every other area of life.

Reflect on your relationship with the small things like food, movies, entertainment, and other desires. Are they doorways to deeper issues? The path forward requires honest self-examination. Can we receive whatever is offered with genuine gratitude, or do we constantly focus on what's wrong or missing?

When we recognize these patterns, we're not doomed to continue in them. God's grace is sufficient to transform even our most mundane daily habits into opportunities for spiritual growth and worship.

One day in prayer, a simple exchange crystallized this truth for me in a way I hope will encourage you:

Lord, why do I sin?

Because you are human and fallen.

Lord, how do I stop sinning?

You move closer to a relationship with your Creator, God.

The answer to mastering our appetites isn't found in willpower alone, but in drawing near to God. As we grow closer to Him, His Spirit transforms our desires from the inside out.

Takeaway

Reflect honestly on your relationship with food and other daily pleasures. Are there areas where you've developed an insatiable appetite for things to be exactly your way? Do your preferences serve you, or have you become enslaved to them? Consider how you respond when things aren't prepared to your specifications, at restaurants, in your home, when others are serving you.

Remember that God created all things good, and He calls us to receive them with thanksgiving. There's nothing spiritual about rejecting quality or refinement, but there's also nothing godly about making idols of our preferences. The goal is to enjoy God's gifts fully while holding them lightly, to appreciate excellence without demanding it, and to use even our refined tastes as opportunities for worship rather than pride.

Examine whether your daily habits with food are contributing to your spiritual effectiveness or hindering it. Are you taking care of your body as the temple of the Holy Spirit? Are you practicing the self-control that strengthens your character for bigger challenges? Most importantly, are you receiving even your daily bread with gratitude, recognizing that every good gift comes from above?

A Closing Prayer

Lord, thank You so much for the wonderful gifts You've given us, the gift of delicacies and pleasures. Help us to receive them with worship and thanksgiving. Bring to light anything in my life that has become an idol or a sinful preference. Let me put all things into subjection under You, so that I can remain in control of my passions, pleasures, and desires, and maintain my focus to worship You. In Jesus' name, Amen.

Chapter 18
Love, Sex, Marriage, and Family

In Letter 18, Screwtape instructs Wormwood on how to distort humanity's understanding of love, marriage, and sexuality by promoting a romanticized, emotion-driven view that prioritizes fleeting feelings over covenant commitment. Here's the demonic strategy, convince humans that being "in love" is the only respectable ground for marriage, and that marriage must serve this feeling. If the romantic emotions fade, then obviously the marriage has failed and should be dissolved. This creates a culture where divorce becomes expected when couples hit rough patches.

The truth is both more complex and more beautiful. The feeling of being in love is the fruit of a good marriage, not the root. When we reverse this order, we build on sand instead of rock. God's design for love and marriage transcends mere emotion. This isn't about dismissing joy and passion but about understanding what serves as the foundation versus what flows as the fruit.

Lewis addresses love and marriage extensively in his letters, and these concepts are so rich that we'll unpack them across two chapters. This chapter focuses on God's design for sex and marriage specifically, while the next chapter explores the broader nature of divine love and how it applies to all our relationships.

Scripture

"Therefore a man shall leave his father and mother and be joined to his wife, and they shall become one flesh. This is a great mystery, but I speak concerning Christ and the church." - Ephesians 5:31-32 (NKJV)

God's Design for Sex and Love

Lewis presents the only two Christian options regarding sexuality: "complete abstinence" for the unmarried and "unmitigated monogamy" for the married. The demonic realm works tirelessly to undermine both standards, and they've now become deeply embedded cultural norms. Culture mocks these ideas. Movies and television normalize sex outside of marriage. Living together before marriage is expected. Pornography is everywhere. And divorce? No big deal, just move on to the next relationship.

Complete abstinence means not engaging in sexual activity outside of marriage. This has become so countercultural that many Christians struggle to embrace it, but it serves a crucial purpose. When you're committed to abstinence, you naturally prioritize finding the right spouse. You can't indefinitely delay marriage while "testing the waters" because the sexual tension creates urgency.

Here's where the demonic strategy becomes clear, if you can get people to engage in casual sex, you remove the natural tendency to prioritize marriage. Sometimes you don't feel the need to get married when you're already getting laid. I've seen countless Christian couples dating for years, unable to decide if they should marry. The truth? They're already sleeping together. Because their sexual needs are being met, there's no urgency to make the hard decisions about commitment. They coast indefinitely in this in-between state.

But when couples practice genuine abstinence, something powerful happens. They're forced to evaluate their relationship based on character, compatibility, life goals, and genuine affection rather than sexual chemistry. And because the sexual tension remains unresolved, they're motivated to move toward marriage.

The wise sequence looks like this: Pursue wisdom. Understand what marriage really is. Pursue dating opportunities with people who know and love the Lord. Date someone of good character who shares your faith and life vision. If the Lord directs, build both the feeling and commitment of love. Then enter into a marriage covenant and consummate that marriage. When you get this order right, you create the best foundation for lasting joy.

Unmitigated monogamy means total faithfulness to your spouse, not just physically but emotionally and mentally as well. You pour all of your sexual energy, romantic attention, and intimate affection into this one relationship. This concentrated focus creates an intensity and depth that casual relationships can never achieve.

Unity Not Competition

Here we encounter one of the profound mysteries of Christian marriage, how two independent people can become genuinely unified without losing their individual identity. When both partners are genuinely seeking each other's good, something remarkable happens in the day-to-day life of marriage.

This isn't about losing yourself or becoming codependent. It's about discovering that love multiplies rather than divides. When I fight for my wife's happiness and she fights for mine, we both win. When we're constantly looking out for each other's interests, nobody gets neglected because we have two people committed to ensuring that both parties flourish.

Here's how it works practically: Because I love you, I actually get joy when you're doing well. My satisfaction becomes wired to your satisfaction. And if we're both doing this for each other, I don't need to look out for my own needs as much because my spouse is looking out for me. My wife is loving me, caring for me, and I'm not suffering from neglecting myself because she's watching out for me too.

The practical applications are endless. Where should we live? What color should we paint the walls? How should we spend our money? When both people are genuinely more interested in blessing their spouse than getting their own way, these decisions become opportunities for joy rather than sources of conflict.

This is why Paul calls marriage "a mystery that speaks of Christ and the church" (Eph. 5:31-32). Just as Jesus found His greatest glory in laying down His life for the church, and just as the church finds its purpose in bringing glory to Christ, marriage provides a living illustration of how love works in the kingdom of God. It's not about sacrifice in the sense of loss but about discovering that true fulfillment comes through seeking the good of another.

Love Multiplies to Family

When this kind of covenant love is working properly between a husband and wife, something beautiful and natural occurs: children. Lewis observed that God "has also made the offspring dependent on the parents and given the parents an impulse to support it, thus producing the family, which is like the organism, only worse, for the members are more distinct yet also united in a more conscious and responsible way. The whole thing turns out to be simply one more device for dragging in love."

The same dynamic that allows a husband to find joy in his wife's happiness becomes even more pronounced when they become parents. Watch a mother instinctively put herself in harm's way to protect her child, or a father work multiple jobs to provide for his family's needs. This isn't a burdensome duty, it's love expressing itself in its most natural form.

Sexual desire and affection between a man and woman bring about children, which leads to an entirely new type of love. The joy that parents find in caring for their children, in seeing them grow and thrive, in making sacrifices for their well-being, represents the multiplication of the same love that characterizes a good marriage. It's not that the parents love each other less; it's that their capacity for love has expanded to encompass these new little image-bearers of God.

Children also provide one of the clearest pictures of how godly love operates. Parents don't love their children because those children have earned it or because they're getting something in return. They love them simply because they have been given them to steward. This models the unconditional nature of God's love for us and reinforces the covenant nature of all healthy relationships.

The family unit becomes a training ground where children learn what love looks like in practice. They see their parents fighting for each other rather than with each other. They experience what it means to be cherished, protected, and provided for. They learn that love involves both tender affection and sacrificial commitment. This preparation equips them to one day create their own marriages and families, perpetuating God's design through the generations.

The forgiveness you extend to your spouse is not merely an act of grace; it is a living testament to the forgiveness you have received from God. If we desire to raise children who walk in the way of Christ, how can we expect them to embrace His love and mercy if they witness bitterness and unforgiveness in the very heart of their home? Divorce often leaves deep and lasting wounds in children, yet many couples who profess Christ at the center of their lives remain estranged, not for lack of love, but for lack of forgiveness. To follow Christ is to forgive as He forgave, even when it costs us.

Satan hates this progression because he recognizes how powerfully it reflects God's character and multiplies His influence in the world. Every strong marriage is a testimony to the gospel. Every healthy family is a small picture of the kingdom of God. Every child raised in this environment becomes equipped to carry forward God's design for human relationships.

How the Enemy Attacks

Understanding marriage and family as reflections of God's character helps us recognize why they're under such intense spiritual attack. Here's how the demonic realm works to undermine God's design:

Normalizing Divorce

Jesus gave the biblical ground for divorce, sexual immorality (Matt. 19:9). Yet we live in a culture where divorce has become normalized, even within the church. Divorce is sometimes necessary, but we've leaned toward normalizing it, and that is not good.

Making Abstinence Seem Impossible

The demonic has programmed culture to make complete abstinence feel ridiculous. Young believers face constant pressure, everyone around them is sexually active, and they're told they're missing out. The enemy convinces believers that purity is impossible, that "everyone's doing it," and that God's design is outdated. But this is a lie.

Redefining Love as Only a Feeling

Satan tries to cross the wires by making the feeling of love the root of marriage instead of the fruit. The feeling of being in love is the fruit of a good marriage, not the root. When the spark fades, the enemy whispers that the marriage has failed. But remember what marriage actually is, a covenant commitment that can rekindle the spark.

Exploiting Vulnerable Seasons

Married couples go through seasons where feelings fade, pressures mount, and passion feels distant. These are precisely when external temptations become most appealing. When life strains the relationship, attractive alternatives seem to appear everywhere. These aren't coincidences, they're strategic attacks designed to exploit vulnerability.

Undermining Physical Intimacy

God created the sexual relationship for bonding. The one-flesh union has supernatural power to recalibrate hearts and minds toward each other. The enemy creates distance through exhaustion, resentment, shame, or neglect. When couples stop being physically intimate, they lose one of their strongest defenses.

Preventing the Gospel Witness

The ultimate goal is to prevent marriages from displaying God's character to a watching world. When marriages fail and sexual relationships become casual, the gospel itself appears less credible.

Strong Christian marriages serve as powerful testimonies to God's covenant love.

Takeaway

God has a unique and beautiful plan for human relationships, love, sex, marriage, and family. But Satan has strategies to distort and corrupt every one of these gifts. He works to replace covenant commitment with fleeting feelings, to normalize divorce, to make sexual purity seem impossible, and to convince us that love is about competition rather than unity.

Walking in God's wisdom is difficult. Not having sex before marriage takes work. Sexual temptation is real. Marriage requires constant effort. But God's design, when we follow it, creates joy and blessings that surpass anything the world can offer.

Your relationships are under spiritual attack precisely because they matter so much in God's kingdom. Expect challenges, prepare for warfare, but trust in God's beautiful design.

A Closing Prayer

Lord, thank You for the gift of marriage and the beautiful design You have for love, sex, and family. Help me to understand how I can live my life in a way that honors Your design, leading to Your glory and my joy. Give me strength when it's difficult, wisdom when it's unclear, and courage to care more about what You think and what You say than what culture or others would have me do. In Jesus' name, Amen.

Chapter 19
Pick Your Love, Love Your Pick

In the previous chapter, we explored God's design for marriage and the one-flesh union. We saw how love in marriage operates on principles that confound worldly thinking. Now we zoom out to understand the broader foundation that makes marriage work, the nature of divine love itself and how it applies to all our relationships.

At the heart of spiritual warfare lies a profound mystery that has confounded the demonic realm since before creation, why would an all-powerful God genuinely love weak, fallen creatures? This question reveals the fundamental difference between divine thinking and every worldview built purely on self-interest. When genuine sacrificial love appears in the world, it exposes the bankruptcy of philosophies that can only comprehend relationships in terms of power, control, or mutual benefit.

This chapter explores why divine love remains incomprehensible to those who operate on purely selfish principles, and how that incomprehension shapes both demonic tactics and human responses to authentic goodness. More importantly, it reveals practical wisdom for navigating the spiritual neutrality of our circumstances, ensuring that our experiences draw us closer to God rather than away from Him.

Scripture

"Love is patient and kind; love does not envy or boast; it is not arrogant or rude. It does not insist on its own way; it is not irritable or resentful; it does not rejoice at wrongdoing, but rejoices with the truth. Love bears all things, believes all things, hopes all things, endures all things. Love never ends. As for prophecies, they will pass away; as for tongues, they will cease; as for knowledge, it will pass away." - 1 Corinthians 13:1-8.

The Mystery of Love

Why did God create humanity? This question lies at the heart of one of the most revealing moments in Screwtape's correspondence. The senior demon becomes concerned that he may have committed demonic heresy by repeatedly acknowledging something their worldview simply cannot accommodate, "He really loves those little vermin."

The demonic worldview operates on what we might call zero-sum principles, for one to win, another must lose. They understand conquest, domination, and self-advancement, but they cannot comprehend a love that finds genuine joy in another's welfare. In their thinking, every relationship is fundamentally competitive. If you're happy, I must be losing something. If you succeed, it must be at my expense. This is the culture of hell, a dog-eat-dog world where love is literally a contradiction in terms.

But this is where the magnificent design of divine love becomes clear. God created us in His image with a specific purpose, to glorify Him and enjoy Him forever. Here's the revolutionary insight, the very thing that brings God the most glory is also the thing that brings us the most satisfaction. We are like small mirrors designed to reflect God's character, and in doing so, we become fully what we were made to be.

This design creates win-win scenarios where God's glory and human flourishing increase together. Love is not a zero-sum game. Let me unpack what this means practically:

When I love my wife, I'm free to genuinely care for her well-being for two reasons. First, I find joy in seeing her succeed, thrive, and flourish. Her happiness becomes my happiness. Second, she reciprocates by looking out for me, caring for my needs, and blessing me. We both benefit. This is how God's love works too.

God loves us and looks out for us for two reasons. First, He finds joy in seeing His children succeed, do well, and flourish. Like any good father, He delights in our well-being. Second, when we worship Him and give Him glory, that honors Him. We can't bless God the way He blesses us, but our worship and obedience bring Him glory.

This mutual benefit of love existed even before the foundation of the world. Lewis hints at this when Screwtape mentions "a certain episode about a cross" discussed before humanity's creation. God's eternal love for us in Christ was the master plan of humanity's narrative. God's redemptive story and His picture of love were so great that He installed it in humanity itself. He gave humans the ability and calling to love, and when they do (though often they don't), it reflects His own character.

This principle makes no sense to minds that operate purely on self-interest. Those who cannot comprehend genuine sacrifice respond with suspicion and hostility. As Screwtape expresses it, they're constantly asking, "If we could only find out what He is really up to!"

They cannot accept that love might exist without ulterior motives because their entire worldview is built on the assumption that everyone acts only for personal gain.

I encountered this attitude firsthand while working with a food pantry in New York City. We operated one of the city's largest private food pantries, funded entirely by donations and staffed by volunteers who genuinely wanted to serve the poor. Yet we faced vicious attacks on our character and motives. Critics insisted we must be getting something out of it, that we had hidden agendas, that no one does good simply because they care for others.

The energy and hostility of these accusations revealed something deeper than simple skepticism. The existence of authentic love and service threatens the fundamental assumptions of those who have chosen to live only for themselves. This is why you'll often see the most intense attacks leveled not against obvious evildoers, but against those who are genuinely trying to do good. Authentic goodness exposes the emptiness of purely selfish worldviews, and those committed to such philosophies feel compelled to explain away or destroy what they cannot understand.

The Neutrality Principle

This understanding of how love multiplies rather than divides reveals something crucial about Satan's strategy. Because God designed love to work through win-win scenarios, because He created good gifts that genuinely bless us while bringing Him glory, the demonic realm faces a significant limitation, they cannot simply eliminate these gifts. Love, beauty, pleasure, knowledge, relationships, these are woven into the fabric of creation itself. Satan cannot destroy them.

So, what can he do? He twists them. He takes what God designed for our flourishing and our joy, and he corrupts it to serve his purposes. He cannot make love cease to exist, but he can distort it into lust or codependency. He cannot eliminate the pleasure of food, but he can twist it into gluttony or idolatry. He cannot destroy the gift of ambition, but he can corrupt it into pride or workaholism.

This is why Screwtape, with remarkable candor, tells Wormwood to stop asking whether any particular thing is good or bad for their purposes. As he puts it, "Nothing matters at all except the tendency of a given state of mind, in given circumstances, to move a particular patient at a particular moment nearer to the Enemy or nearer to us."

This leads us to a revolutionary insight that should transform how you approach every area of life, most of the experiences and opportunities you encounter are spiritually neutral. They can serve either to draw you closer to God or pull you away from Him. The question isn't whether the circumstance itself is inherently good or bad, but whether you're using it to grow in love and godliness or allowing it to feed selfishness and pride.

Let's examine how this works in practice. Consider education. Pursuing knowledge can draw you closer to God as you discover the intricacies of His creation and develop discernment. But education can also pull you away from God if it breeds pride, replaces wisdom with mere information, or indoctrinates you with worldviews that contradict Scripture.

Political involvement offers another example. Engaging in civic life can beautifully express love for your neighbor and the pursuit of justice. But politics can also become idolatrous, dividing believers over secondary issues or causing you to place ultimate hope in human institutions rather than God's kingdom.

The same applies to career success, artistic pursuits, recreation, and countless other areas. God created these as gifts to be enjoyed and used for His glory, but our fallen nature tends to turn gifts into gods.

This brings us to the most important application, the experience of falling in love. As Lewis puts it, the question isn't whether love itself is good or bad, but whether someone uses it to move closer to God or further away.

Romantic feelings can draw someone closer to God by teaching about sacrifice, commitment, and finding joy in another's welfare. The experience of caring deeply for someone else provides a taste of how God cares for us. It can motivate personal growth and expand thinking beyond selfish desires. But those same feelings can pull someone away from God when they become idolatrous, when they're built purely on physical attraction, or when they lead to relationships that undermine faith. When feelings become the foundation for major life decisions, when someone abandons wisdom because they're "in love," then love becomes destructive rather than beneficial.

The key insight is this, many aspects of life are spiritually neutral. What matters is how you respond to them, what you build on them, and whether you use them to grow in wisdom and godliness or allow them to compromise your spiritual priorities.

Practical Wisdom for Love and Marriage

Since romantic feelings can lead in either direction, we need practical wisdom to ensure they draw us closer to God rather than away from Him. Let's step back from analyzing the spiritual realm and focus on specific, actionable guidance. Here's how to apply the neutrality principle to relationships.

Answer the Two Most Important Questions First

You'll only face two truly crucial decisions in your lifetime, who is your God, and who is your spouse? The first determines your eternal destiny, while the second shapes virtually everything about your earthly experience (Including lineage). Both deserve your most careful consideration.

When it comes to choosing a spouse, remember that you're not just looking for someone who creates butterflies in your stomach. You're choosing a partner for the most important human relationship of your life, someone who will either help you become more like Christ or make spiritual growth significantly more difficult.

Have the Hard Conversations Early

If you find yourself developing strong feelings for someone, use that attraction as motivation for deeper evaluation rather than the basis for major decisions. The excitement of new love should drive you toward greater intentionality, not less.

Can you have meaningful conversations about money, debt, and financial planning? These discussions reveal character, wisdom, and compatibility in ways that romantic dinners never will. Share your dreams about career, ministry, and family. Explore your philosophies about raising children, serving the church, and using your time and resources.

These conversations serve a crucial purpose. If your relationship can't survive honest discussions about real-life issues, then it's built on nothing more substantial than romantic feelings. But if examining these realities deepens your appreciation for this person and strengthens your desire to build a life together, then you're discovering the foundation that can support a lasting marriage.

Build Character-Based Attraction

Physical attraction and emotional connection matter, but they must be built on something deeper. Look for evidence of spiritual maturity, integrity under pressure, kindness to those who can't help them, and commitment to growth and truth.

Watch how they treat service workers, handle disappointment, respond to correction, and talk about former relationships. These behaviors reveal character far more clearly than romantic gestures or passionate declarations ever could.

Maintain Physical Boundaries

One of the most practical ways to ensure romantic feelings serve God's purposes rather than undermining them is by maintaining sexual purity before marriage. This isn't just about following rules, it's about creating the conditions for wise decision-making.

When sexual intimacy is removed from a dating relationship, you're forced to build a connection on conversation, shared experiences, mutual service, and genuine compatibility. Physical boundaries protect your ability to think clearly about long-term compatibility rather than being clouded by powerful physical and emotional experiences.

Continue Investing After Marriage

If you're already married, the same principles apply to maintaining spiritual direction in your relationship. Continue investing in what brought you together initially. Make regular time for just the two of you, putting away distractions and focusing on each other.

Discuss your spiritual growth together, your goals and dreams, and how you can better support each other's relationship with God. Don't neglect physical intimacy; the one-flesh union God designed strengthens the covenant bond between husband and wife.

Focus on Becoming the Right Person

Finally, invest as much energy in becoming someone who would contribute to a godly marriage as you do in finding the right partner. The same sacrificial love that characterizes God's relationship with us should mark our relationships with each other.

This requires daily choices to prioritize your spouse's spiritual welfare, speak truth in love even when difficult, forgive quickly and seek forgiveness humbly, and view marriage as a ministry that displays God's character to a watching world.

Takeaway

The mystery of God's love reveals that our ultimate purpose and greatest joy perfectly align. We were created to glorify God by enjoying Him forever, and this design creates win-win scenarios that confound those who think only in terms of competition and self-interest. Love is not a zero-sum game.

Recognize that most of your circumstances are spiritually neutral. What matters isn't the circumstances themselves but whether you're using them to grow closer to God or allowing them to pull you away from Him. This is especially critical when it comes to romantic feelings and relationships.

Use attraction as motivation for a deeper evaluation of character and compatibility rather than making it the foundation for major life decisions. The enemy's goal is to use your relationships to undermine your faith. Counter this by approaching every relationship with the question, how can this draw me and others closer to God?

When you keep that question central, even your most intimate relationships become means of grace that strengthen your faith and advance God's kingdom in the world.

A Closing Prayer

Lord, help me to understand the profound truth that love is not a competition but a multiplication. Teach me to find joy in the welfare of others, just as You find joy in blessing us. Give me wisdom to recognize when my circumstances are drawing me closer to You or pulling me away. In all my relationships, may I reflect Your character and point others to Your love. In Jesus' name, Amen.

Chapter 20
When Lust Rages

In the previous two chapters, we explored God's design for marriage and the nature of divine love. We established that complete abstinence outside marriage and unmitigated monogamy within it reflect God's blueprint for human sexuality. Now we need to understand the sophisticated spiritual warfare that makes living out this design so challenging. Sexual temptation represents one of the most intense battlegrounds in the Christian life, but here's the encouraging truth we must grasp from the outset: victory is possible.

The demonic realm works tirelessly to use sexuality for our destruction, targeting not just individual lives but entire families and future generations. As Screwtape observes with dark satisfaction, the unhappiness produced by sexual sin proves "of a very lasting and exquisite kind." This chapter exposes the lies that keep men enslaved to sexual temptation, reveals how culture programs our desires, and provides practical wisdom for walking in freedom rather than bondage.

A word about this chapter's focus, while we write this book for both men and women, this chapter, as Lewis does, speaks more directly to male sexual temptation. Men drive much of the world's sexual brokenness in culture, from pornography to exploitation. When men gain victory over sexual sin, families flourish and communities become healthier. We invite our female readers to understand the specific battles men face, recognizing that male sexual discipline benefits everyone.

Scripture

"For this is the will of God, your sanctification: that you abstain from sexual immorality; that each one of you know how to control his own body in holiness and honor, not in the passion of lust like the Gentiles who do not know God." - 1 Thessalonians 4:3-5

The Demonic Lie About Victory

One of the most encouraging truths about sexual temptation is also one of the most carefully hidden, breakthrough can and does happen. Screwtape himself admits that God sometimes puts "an end to direct attacks" on a person's chastity. Many men struggling with sexual sin believe they're trapped in a battle they can never win, but this represents a fundamental deception designed to keep them enslaved.

The belief that the only way to get rid of sexual temptation is by yielding to it stands as perhaps the enemy's most effective weapon. Most don't think this overtly, but they think subconsciously, "This temptation is never going away. I just have to learn to manage it." Or sometimes, "This is just the way I am." This diabolical lie doesn't just discourage us from pursuing victory. It also supports much of the sexual confusion that's rampant in our culture today. The core foundation of the LGBTQ movement for instance is, "I was born this way, and I can't change it." This represents one of the most demonic expressions in human culture because it not only says "I'm going to give in to this sin," but takes it further, "I'm going to embrace it, have pride about it, and create an identity around it." One that God didn't create.

But here's the truth that can set you free. Whatever you're struggling with is something you can conquer. The battle may be difficult. You may need help, strong accountability, and people in your corner supporting you and cheering for you. But victory is absolutely possible.

If you're struggling with sexual addiction or pornography, know that genuine help exists. Resources like the Pure Desire Ministry and specifically their Conqueror Series provide group-based or individual biblical, practical, and psychological tools for breaking free. You don't have to fight alone, and you don't have to settle for simply managing sin. God offers real victory, real freedom, and real transformation. The lie that you're powerless is exactly that, a lie!

Who Decides What's Attractive?

Understanding sexual temptation requires recognizing that we're not just fighting individual battles. We're engaging in spiritual warfare that operates at the highest levels of culture. Demonic forces don't just tempt individuals day by day, they work at a much higher level, manipulating what society considers beautiful, desirable, and sexually attractive. They subtly shift cultural standards through entertainment, media, and platforms of influence.

Even decades ago, observers noted that "small circles of popular artists, dressmakers, actresses, and advertisers" determine what becomes fashionable and desirable. This is exactly what we see today with social media influencers, fashion designers, entertainment executives, and advertising agencies. The people setting these trends typically work in places that function as demonic strongholds. Major cities, where pride and vanity fuel entire industries, become epicenters for programming what society finds attractive.

Here's what makes this particularly dangerous. It's never godly people setting these trends. It's always those trying to push boundaries, break norms, and seek attention through rebellion. The least healthy and least virtuous people end up determining what "sexy" looks like, and Christian men fall victim because these influences saturate every aspect of culture.

Consider how dramatically standards have shifted over recent decades. From extremely thin women like Twiggy to voluptuous figures like Anna Nicole Smith. Even Renaissance paintings show how different eras promoted vastly different ideals of female beauty. The question we must ask is, who's driving these changes and why?

Today we're witnessing an even more dramatic shift. The promotion of transgender individuals as sexually desirable is being normalized. There's truth in the saying, "What we tolerate will soon be celebrated." The demonic realm knows this, which is why every counterfeit of God's design first battles simply to be tolerated.

This manipulation creates what we might call "sexual inflation." Just as economic inflation requires more money to buy the same goods, sexual inflation requires increasingly exotic experiences to achieve the same satisfaction. When someone engages in casual sex repeatedly, their expectations escalate continuously. They need more variety, more intensity, more novelty to feel satisfied. This creates a devastating cycle where virtuous, godly partners become less appealing by comparison.

Here's the deception, no one lists their number of sexual partners on their resume. High body counts aren't admirable. They are a trail of lies, deceit and bad decisions legitimized as necessary sexual experience. Instead of uniting couples, sexual history creates comparison and judgment that transforms intimacy into a performance to be evaluated. No married couple raising children with Christ at the center benefits from sexual experience before marriage.

Two Types That Capture the Male Imagination

Lewis identifies two types of women that capture male attention, and understanding this distinction proves crucial for Christian men. The terrestrial Venus represents the woman who lives according to God's design. She's down to earth in mind, body, and spirit. You might find her tending her garden, pursuing the virtues God designed her to have. She's the Proverbs 31 woman who lives as God intended, focusing on family and building her home rather than career ambitions and social media followings.

The infernal Venus, by contrast, embodies exotic, performance-driven sexuality. She's hot like the fires of hell because that's where she is, sadly, heading. She represents forbidden love, sexual prowess, and the pursuit of increasingly exotic experiences. Men become consumed by the drive for this kind of sexual fulfillment. They seek pleasure but, in the end, will find only self-ruin. This is the woman described in Proverbs 30:20, "She eats and wipes her mouth and says, 'I have done no wickedness.' "She consumes men and then acts as if nothing has happened, leaving destruction in her wake.

While every man naturally experiences some attraction to both types, the infernal Venus poisons appreciation for the terrestrial one. Sexual inflation makes the godly woman seem boring by comparison, even though she represents everything that would actually bring lasting joy and satisfaction. The demonic strategy proves brilliant, even if Christian men avoid premarital sex, they can still be led to marry the wrong woman because they pursued the wrong kind of woman and for the wrong reasons.

When Fire Escapes the Fireplace

Sex is one of the most powerful aspects of human experience. That's why God used it as the mechanism for creating life. It's so powerful that it literally brings human beings into existence. Understanding sex requires recognizing that it operates like fire in your home.

Fire serves wonderful purposes when properly contained. In a fireplace, it provides heat, beauty, and atmosphere. It warms your family and creates celebration. It's incredibly valuable when it stays where it belongs. But fire requires very little to escape its boundaries. Once it does, it instantly brings destruction rather than blessing. Even a tiny ember outside its designed place will start burning things down. What was meant to beautify your life quickly becomes an agent of destruction.

Sex operates according to exactly the same principle. Within what God designed, between a man and woman in marriage for life, it's beautiful. It creates intimacy, facilitates procreation, builds covenant bonds, and brings tremendous joy. But any distortion, any change from God's design turns it into fire outside a fireplace. Rather than beautifying your life, it burns everything to the ground.

The destructive power of misused sexuality extends far beyond individual lives. It tears apart families, destroys communities, and creates massive social problems affecting entire generations.

"For this is the will of God, your sanctification: that you abstain from sexual immorality; that each one of you know how to control his own body in holiness and honor, not in the passion of lust like the Gentiles who do not know God; that no one transgress and wrong his brother in this matter, because

the Lord is an avenger in all these things, as we told you beforehand and solemnly warned you. For God has not called us for impurity, but in holiness." - 1 Thessalonians 4:3-7.

One of the Great Evils of Our Time

As you may have noticed in reading this book, we are quite passionate about standing for life. While we've mentioned the topic of abortion a few times already, we'd like to address here in light is the subject of sexual sin. The abortion industry, or more accurately, the child sacrifice industry, represents one of the most heartbreaking consequences of abandoning God's design for sexuality. God creates life at conception. Science has even captured the remarkable moment when sperm penetrates the egg, and a corona of light appears around it. Another profound example of God saying, "Let there be Light."

Every year, millions of God's creations are destroyed because of men's and women's sexual choices and desire for lifestyle convenience. The great deception occurs when this gets framed as "reproductive rights" rather than what it actually is, the taking of innocent human life. The fervor behind the abortion movement stems from a single source, the belief that women are the ultimate decision-makers for the life inside them, with the Creator having no part in the equation.

The abortion industry reveals how deeply sexual sin corrupts, not just individual lives, but entire societies. What begins as misuse of God's gift of sex ends in the systematic destruction of the most innocent and vulnerable human beings.

If you've had an abortion or encouraged someone to have one, know that there is grace. There is forgiveness. There is healing. God's mercy extends even to our deepest failures and greatest regrets. But we must also stand firmly against the cultural forces that normalize this evil and lead people into decisions that will haunt them for years to come. The compassionate response is both to offer grace to those who have been deceived and to speak truth that protects others from the same devastating path.

The Two Most Important Questions

You'll face two truly crucial decisions in your lifetime. Who is your God, and who is your spouse? The first determines your eternal destiny. The second shapes virtually everything about your earthly experience and your lineage. Both deserve your most careful consideration.

This explains why some Christian men successfully avoid premarital sex but still end up in terrible marriages. They become so focused on "don't have sex before marriage" that they overlook whether their partner has good character, genuine faith, or even desires physical intimacy at all. They win the battle against premarital sex but lose the war because they haven't built their relationship on the proper foundation.

The solution involves both immediate purity and long-term wisdom. Maintain physical boundaries that protect your ability to think clearly about character and compatibility. Use the discipline required for sexual purity as motivation to evaluate yourself, your relationship, and your potential spouse carefully. Remember that successfully avoiding premarital sex doesn't guarantee a happy marriage. You still need to do the work walking wisely from singlehood into marriage.

When two people pursue each other with God at the center and then agree to be passionate and open with each other, the pull toward sexual sin diminishes both before and after marriage. Dating can be pure and open as it lays a solid foundation. And the joy of sex within marriage can be an expression of covenant love and mutual service.

So, answer both questions rightly, and you set yourself up for a lifetime of flourishing. Get either one wrong and you'll spend years dealing with the consequences.

Takeaway

Sexual sin destroys more than we admit. It fractures future marriages, corrupts our view of others, trains us to crave what will never satisfy, and separates us from the intimacy God designed. The battle for sexual purity is unrelenting. Many reading this have fought for years, stumbled repeatedly, and wondered if freedom is even possible. This does not have to be your story forever. God offers real transformation. Not always easy, and seldom quick, but real. Godly relationships are possible. The joy of sex within covenant marriage is worth fighting for. Victory may require painful honesty, deep accountability, tearing down years of programming, and walking a harder road than you wanted. But at the end of that road is freedom. True freedom. The fire that's been destroying your life can become the warmth that blesses your marriage. Not because you're strong enough, but because Christ is. The battle is fierce, but God's grace is fiercer. Fight for that. It's worth it.

A Closing Prayer

Lord, thank you for the gifts of marriage and sex. I need Your strength to overcome my fleshly desires and walk in purity. Help me pursue the relationships You want for me the way You want. Cleanse me, Lord, and renew me through Your forgiveness, that I may live virtuously in Christ. In His holy name, Amen.

Chapter 21
The Deadly Trap of "Mine"

In this letter, C. S. Lewis shifts focus from sexual temptation to something that might seem far less significant. The petty irritation we feel when our daily plans get disrupted. At first glance, this appears to be a minor detour, but Lewis reveals something profound. While we're busy fighting the obvious battles against major sins, the enemy often slips in through the back door with an attack that seems almost trivial by comparison.

The trap Lewis exposes is deceptively simple. The belief that our time, our plans, our resources, and ultimately our lives belong to us. This assumption feels so natural, so obviously true, that we rarely question it. Yet this single lie opens the door to a form of selfishness that can poison every relationship, rob us of joy, and separate us from God's purposes for our lives. When we operate from the premise that we own anything at all, we set ourselves up for constant frustration and spiritual defeat.

Scripture

"The earth is the Lord's and the fullness thereof, the world and those who dwell therein, for he has founded it upon the seas and established it upon the rivers." - Psalm 24:1-2

The Sin of Peevishness

Picture yourself on an ordinary Tuesday evening. You've planned a quiet walk in the park or some uninterrupted time to read. Then it happens, the neighbor catches you at the mailbox and launches into a twenty-minute story about their doctor's visit. Or an old friend drops by unannounced. Or the bus runs late, throwing off your entire schedule. That familiar surge of frustration rises in your chest. Your evening is shot. Your plans are ruined. And you find yourself genuinely irritated that your time has been stolen from you.

The word Lewis uses to describe this reaction is "peevishness," and it captures something both petty and profound. We're not talking about righteous anger over injustice. We're talking about the childish indignation we feel when the world has the audacity to inconvenience us. Yet somehow, we slip into operating as though every minute belongs to us by right.

Lewis provides one of the most powerful illustrations for reframing this entire mindset. Let's explore it the way Screwtape did. Imagine that Jesus Christ himself appeared to you in person right now. Picture him walking into your living room or meeting you on the street. You would be overwhelmed, falling down in worship, ready to cancel every plan you had for the day.

Now imagine that the Lord gives you an assignment. "I want you to spend this entire day with that elderly gentleman sitting over there," he might say. "Just listen to his stories about his life." Would you hesitate for even a second? Would you mention that you had other plans? Of course not. You would consider it the highest honor imaginable. You would be thrilled to receive such a direct assignment from your Savior. You would cancel the most important meeting without a moment's regret. In fact, if Jesus were to say, "I'll be with you for twenty-four hours, but right now take a thirty-minute break for yourself," you might actually dread those thirty minutes, being pulled away from the magnificent opportunity to serve Jesus directly.

When you think about it this way, the shameful nature of our daily irritations becomes crystal clear. Every interruption, every unexpected encounter, every deviation from our plans could very well be an assignment from the Lord himself. That chatty neighbor who catches you at an inconvenient time, that unexpected visitor, that delayed bus that puts you in conversation with a stranger, all could be divine appointments that we're missing because we're too focused on protecting our "personal time." If we truly accept that every minute belongs to the Lord and is given to us to steward, our entire perspective would shift.

From Selfishness to Stewardship

This understanding of ownership typically doesn't come naturally. Most of us have to learn it through a process of maturity that often follows predictable patterns.

Young people naturally tend to be more selfish about time and possessions. Children operate according to what some have humorously called the "Toddler Property Laws": If it's mine, it's mine. If I like it, it's mine. If it's in my hands, it's mine. If I can take it from you, it's mine. If I had it a week ago, it's mine. If it looks just like mine, it's mine. If I was thinking about it, it's mine. If it's broken, it's yours.

While this mindset is amusing in toddlers, it's sobering to recognize how much it persists into adulthood if we resist maturity. Teenagers throw genuine fits when they can't go to their friend's house or when their phone gets taken away. Young adults often approach life assuming their time, energy, and resources are primarily their own. This isn't necessarily a character flaw; it's often simply immaturity.

But we are made in the image of God. Which means we can think, reason, and understand higher purposes. We can comprehend what it means to use our lives and resources to build something bigger than ourselves, to worship the Lord and participate in his kingdom work.

Life has a way of maturing us. Take marriage for instance. It forces us to confront our selfishness in ways we never faced as single people. You can't just decide what to do with your evening without considering someone else. Part of you starts to die in this process, but it's the selfish, immature part that needed to die anyway. When children come into the picture, this process accelerates dramatically. Parents often joke that they can't get three minutes of uninterrupted conversation. Every moment is devoted to caring for others. Yet rather than being a burden, this forced selflessness often brings deeper lasting joy than any self-focused pursuit ever could.

This progression from selfishness to service isn't something to be dreaded; it's the path to true fulfillment. Those who have walked this road don't regret leaving their immaturity behind. They've discovered that life lived for others is far richer than life lived for self.

But this journey reveals something crucial about ownership itself. We naturally have a mindset that says, "This belongs to me, and I have the right to use it however I want for my own benefit." But when we embrace God's perspective, the focus shifts from my ownership to my stewardship. This recognizes that everything ultimately belongs to the Lord, He has simply entrusted certain resources to us to manage on his behalf.

This stewardship mindset allows us to enjoy God's good gifts while holding them with open hands. We can pursue success, own businesses, accumulate wealth, and exercise influence, recognizing that God wants his people to grow in influence and use their resources for His purposes and be salt and light in every area of society.

The Parable of the Talents found in Matthew 25:14-30 illustrates this perfectly. A master entrusts servants with different amounts: five talents to one, two to another, and one to the third. The first two invested their master's money and doubled it. When the master returned, each was commended: "Well done, good and faithful servant." The third servant buried his talent out of fear. When confronted, he was called wicked and lazy. The point is unmistakable, everything we have belongs to our Master, and he expects us to invest it wisely for his purposes.

From Stewardship to Gratitude

Once we understand that everything belongs to God and we're merely stewards, a natural question arises. What are we commanded to do with what He's entrusted to us? The answer reveals the difference between two fundamentally opposed worldviews.

The demonic realm pushes us toward entitlement and accumulation. They whisper, "The one with the most toys wins," turning life into a competition of gathering rather than giving. They want us fixated on what we deserve, what we've earned, what we're owed. This mindset breeds bitterness when we don't receive what we think we're entitled to, and it produces hoarding when we do.

Consider how often we use the word "deserve." "I deserve a break." "I deserve this purchase." "I deserve better treatment." Where does this come from? It's not God. The word carries an assumption that no argument can be made against our claim, that we're entitled to whatever we're demanding. It's overtly selfish, and it kills gratitude.

Gratitude operates from an entirely different premise. When we recognize that we deserve nothing and that every good thing is a gift, blessings become occasions for joy rather than expectations to be met. The wealth we accumulate through work may feel earned, but don't discount God's part in blessing you with skills, opportunities, health, and timing. Every success story involves countless factors beyond our control, the family we were born into, the education we received, the mentors who guided us, the doors that opened at just the right moment.

This is where charity flows naturally from stewardship. When we hold our resources with open hands, recognizing them as God's provision rather than our possession, generosity stops being a burden and becomes a joy. We're not giving away what's ours; we're redirecting what was always God's according to his purposes.

Mark 12:41-44 captures this beautifully. Jesus sat watching people bring their offerings to the temple treasury. Many wealthy people donated large sums. Then a poor widow came and put in two small copper coins, worth almost nothing. Jesus called his disciples over and said, "Truly I tell you, this poor widow has put more into the treasury than all the others. They all gave out of their wealth; but she, out of her poverty, put in everything, all she had to live on."

This widow was charitable in action, and generous in spirit. She understood something the wealthy donors missed. True generosity isn't always measured by the amount given but by the heart behind the gift and the sacrifice it represents. She gave not from her excess but from her trust that God would provide.

There is a sobering reality, we enter this world with nothing and leave with nothing. Job understood when he declared, "Naked I

came from my mother's womb, and naked shall I return" (Job 1:21).
While we're here on earth, we need food, shelter, and resources to
build and serve, but these are provisions from God for the journey, not
the destination itself. The question isn't whether we'll leave it all
behind, we will. The question is whether we'll use it for God's
kingdom while we're here or waste it protecting what was never truly
ours.

Takeaway

This issue sits at the center of a cosmic battle for allegiance.
Both God and Satan are laying claim to every aspect of our lives, but
they operate from fundamentally different positions.

God operates from rightful authority as the Creator and owner
of everything that exists. Scripture makes his ownership clear, Psalm
24:1 says, "The earth is the Lord's and everything in it." Haggai 2:8
says, "The silver is mine and the gold is mine,' declares the Lord of
hosts." This isn't a power grab; this is the rightful owner claiming what
has always been His.

Satan must work through deception and theft. He has no
legitimate claim to anything, so he must convince us to surrender what
belongs to God by making us believe it belongs to us instead. His
strategy is to get us to see ourselves as the rightful owners of our time,
our resources, our bodies, our lives. He is perfectly content to let us
waste our lives in pursuit of temporary pleasures because every
opportunity we miss because we're protecting our personal interests is
a victory for the one who "comes only to steal and kill and destroy."

Until we recognize that nothing in our lives actually belongs to
us, we remain vulnerable to the enemy's primary strategy, getting us to
live as though we were our own gods.

A Closing Prayer

Dear Lord, thank you for all the good and wonderful gifts you have bestowed on me in my life, I am truly grateful. Please help me to be a good servant and steward of my blessings and help me to use them for others. Guide me in charity with my time, wealth, and resources to be a witness of your goodness. Help me grow in maturity every day of my life until my last breath. My heart is filled with gratitude as I praise you. Amen.

Chapter 22
Heaven at Home

In this letter, the patient has fallen in love with a woman of remarkable virtue, and Screwtape is absolutely furious about it. But his rage isn't just about her personal character. It's about the world she comes from; a home so filled with God's presence that it creates what Lewis calls an "impenetrable mystery" to the demonic realm. It's the result of choices, priorities, and daily decisions that build one kind of culture instead of another. It's a matter of following the Lord or giving into the flesh.

The question this letter forces us to ask is simple but profound. What kind of culture are you cultivating in your sphere of influence? Every home, every relationship, every space you occupy regularly is becoming something. It's either becoming a place where God's presence is evident and the enemy has no foothold, or it's becoming something else entirely. This chapter is about how to recognize the difference and what practical steps we can take to cultivate the culture of heaven in our homes, starting today.

Scripture

"But the fruit of the Spirit is love, joy, peace, longsuffering, kindness, goodness, faithfulness, gentleness, self-control. Against such there is no law. And those who are Christ's have crucified the flesh with its passions and desires. If

A Home That Reeks of Heaven

As we've mentioned before, the patient in Lewis's letter has fallen in love. But this isn't just any romance. He's fallen for a woman of remarkable virtue, someone who embodies what Scripture describes in Proverbs 31. She's sweet, kind, and pure in heart, mind, and spirit. Her very presence carries an aroma of heaven itself.

But what really infuriates the demonic realm isn't just this woman's personal virtue. It's the world she comes from, the world she embodies and lives in, the world that surrounds her and that she invites others to share. Her home is filled with plain and simple joy, a deep satisfaction that flows from living in alignment with God's design. This isn't surface-level happiness or forced cheerfulness. It's genuine. People in her household truly love and care for one another. Unity and peace aren't distant ideals but everyday realities.

Lewis describes something extraordinary happening in this home. The house and garden both carry a heavenly quality that's almost tangible. Even the family's pets seem affected by it. Guests who visit for just a weekend leave carrying some of that aroma with them. The gardener, who's only worked there for five years, is beginning to acquire it himself. This creates what Screwtape calls an "impenetrable mystery." A home where demonic forces simply cannot gain a foothold because God's presence is too strong, too real, too evident.

But how does a home like this come to be? We don't know all the specifics of what this family does. What we do know is that something profound is happening. They live in a way that honors God.

They've learned to enjoy the simple blessings of life as gifts from their Father. Scripture tells us that "at his right hand are pleasures forevermore" (Psalm 16:11).

God absolutely delights in seeing His children experience joy and satisfaction. In fact, He's designed us to find deep pleasure in the very activities that make us human: sleeping that refreshes, eating that nourishes and brings people together, playing that creates laughter, praying that connects us to Him, and working that serves others and builds something meaningful. When these everyday activities happen in a home where God is honored, they become more than just routine. They become expressions of worship that fill the atmosphere with heaven's culture.

Filled with the Spirit

How do we create homes like this? What's the foundation that makes such an environment possible? It starts with walking in step with the Holy Spirit. When we believe the gospel, embrace Christ, and allow His Spirit to work in our lives, this kind of culture begins to emerge naturally.

When someone falls in love with a person of genuine virtue, love itself becomes a powerful force against demonic influence. Love, when lived out the way God designed it, embodies virtue and purity that threaten the enemy's work. There's something about true love, whether romantic love between spouses or family love within a household, that demons simply cannot understand or copy. They can twist it or fake it, but they cannot create the real thing.

The fruits of the Spirit (Galatians 5:22–23), aren't just a list of nice qualities we should try to develop. They're the natural result of the

Holy Spirit genuinely working in our lives. Let's look at what each one creates in a home:

Love means genuinely caring for one another, not using each other, or keeping score. It's choosing to serve rather than demanding to be served.

Joy is deep satisfaction that goes beyond circumstances. It's being able to celebrate together even when life is hard, finding reasons to be grateful even in difficulty.

Peace creates an atmosphere where conflict doesn't escalate unnecessarily, where people can disagree without destroying relationships, where calm wins over chaos.

Patience gives family members grace when they fail or struggle, understanding that growth takes time and setbacks are part of life.

Kindness shows up in a thousand small ways: the encouraging word, the helping hand, the thoughtful gesture that says, "I see you and I care."

Goodness pursues what's right and true even when it's inconvenient, creating a moral compass for the household.

Faithfulness builds trust over time through actions that match our words, creating security and stability.

Gentleness handles difficult situations and people with care rather than harshness, especially those who are vulnerable.

Self-control manages emotions and desires rather than being controlled by them, choosing wisdom over impulse.

These aren't traits we develop in isolation. They come as a package deal from being filled with and led by the Spirit. When we walk with God, submit to His Spirit, and live out the gospel in our relationships, these qualities naturally begin to mark our homes. This is what creates an environment where we forgive freely and repent often, where restoration is normal, where unity is valued, and where love covers a multitude of sins.

Identifying and Removing Strongholds

If we want to create homes that reflect heaven's culture, we must be honest about what's giving the enemy access to our spaces. The Bible calls these "strongholds," faulty thought patterns, harmful beliefs, and areas of sin that resist God's truth and give the enemy a foothold in our lives.

The Old Testament gives us a clear example in Judges 6:25-27. God commanded Gideon to tear down his father's altar to a false god before he could effectively serve the Lord and deliver Israel. The lesson is timeless: before public victories can be won, private battles must be fought. We cannot cultivate heaven's culture while maintaining things that give the enemy authority.

"All things originate from God, who is the Creator of everything seen and unseen." (Colossians 1:16). However, when human hearts ascribe undue power, trust, or worship to created things, they can become corrupted and even instruments of spiritual bondage. It is not the physical object but what we project onto it that creates a stronghold. Paul warns, when we exchange "the truth about God for a lie and worship and serve created things rather than the Creator" (Romans 1:25) we open doors to spiritual corruption.

When we elevate possessions, symbols, or comforts above God, or allow fear, superstition, or desire to govern our relationship to them, we create spiritual footholds. They promise comfort, control, or escape, yet ultimately enslave those who trust in them. Understanding these practical strongholds is essential if we are to confront them not merely as moral failings, but as spiritual fortresses that must be torn down through truth, repentance, and God's power.

We are naturally drawn to certain sins through our fallen nature. But when we surrender repeatedly to these temptations and allow patterns to form, we create openings for the demonic to exploit. While the concept of strongholds may sound abstract or ancient, their reality is vividly present in the modern world.

Alcoholism destroys families and self-control, often becoming a gateway that enables other addictions and vices.

Pornography fosters shame, distorts intimacy in marriage, and fuels unhealthy desires and unrealistic expectations that undermine authentic connection.

Drugs enslave body and mind, clouding judgment, damaging relationships, and severing connection with God.

Gambling feeds greed and idolatry, trapping people in cycles of debt and dishonesty as they chase fleeting riches instead of trusting God's provision.

Social media breeds comparison, envy, and distraction, fragmenting attention and quietly eroding peace, joy, and authentic community.

Technology, when unchecked, fosters dependence, isolation, and escapism, distracting from real relationships and spiritual growth.

Occult practices both overt forms such as witchcraft or divination and much more subtle forms such as yoga, meditation, or demonic symbolisms that are dismissed as "cultural" bind the soul to deception and invite spiritual darkness.

Here's a crucial truth, we don't often realize our actions are opening these doors. But God has given us His Word as a guide, calling us to think carefully about our choices and discern whether they honor or dishonor Him.

Begin with honest self-examination. When you're alone, what thoughts and actions draw you in? What do you reach for when you're lonely, stressed, or bored? These reveal where strongholds may have taken root. Father Mike Schmitz observes, "Every sin is an attempt to be happy without God." That's what strongholds promise, happiness, relief, satisfaction, but they deliver only temporary pleasure followed by shame.

Scripture tells us in 2 Corinthians 10:5 that strongholds must be demolished by "taking every thought captive to Christ." Overcoming them requires:

- **Prayer** - Inviting God's power into the battle
- **Repentance** - Turning away from patterns that bind us
- **God's Word** - Immersing ourselves in truth that counters lies
- **Community** - Seeking support from other believers who can help us find freedom

For those caught in addiction cycles, there comes a crossroads where you must choose between continuing in sin or turning wholeheartedly to Jesus. That moment of decision determines whether freedom is possible.

Taking Spiritual Authority

Removing strongholds is essential, but it's only half the battle. We must also learn to take spiritual authority over our homes and actively install the culture of heaven. This is where we move from defense to offense in spiritual warfare.

Dr. Marcus Warner, who has written extensively on spiritual warfare, teaches about two key principles: authority and permission. The enemy can only operate where he has permission, which comes through sin, wounds, or strongholds. But when we exercise our authority in Christ, we can remove that permission and displace demonic influence.

Jesus taught this in Matthew 12:29, "How can anyone enter a strong man's house and plunder his goods, unless he first binds the strong man? Then indeed he may plunder his house." Jesus was explaining that He came to bind Satan and rescue people from his control. In the same way, we have authority in Christ to bind the enemy's influence in our homes and lives.

This isn't about magical rituals or superstition. It's about understanding biblical principles and applying them practically. Consecrating your home means intentionally setting it apart for God's purposes. It starts with repenting of anything that has given the enemy access. This might require identifying specific sins, asking forgiveness, and declaring those doorways closed by the blood of Jesus. It continues with declaring God's purposes for your home. What is your home supposed to be about? What's your mission? What values will guide you? Speaking these truths matters because it establishes spiritual authority.

Then comes the practical work of maintaining an environment that honors God. Fill your home with worship music that cleanses the atmosphere and declares truth. Consider letting the Bible play even while you sleep, allowing God's Word to saturate the environment. Place Scripture on walls where you'll see it regularly. Leave notes of encouragement for one another. Create physical reminders of God's goodness throughout your living space.

Be intentional about what you allow in. Choose entertainment that builds up rather than tears down. Select music that points toward beauty and truth. Fill your bookshelves with books that inspire virtue. Practice forgiveness quickly and thoroughly. Be open and repent often, your household's motto. Learn to laugh together. Find joy in simple pleasures. Celebrate God's goodness in everyday moments. Make your dinner table a place of good conversation, your living room a place of peace, your bedrooms places of genuine rest.

The goal is creating what becomes an impenetrable mystery to demonic forces, a home where God's presence is so evident that the enemy cannot gain ground. This doesn't mean perfection. It means direction. It means consistently choosing to build rather than tear down, to unite rather than divide, to cultivate heaven's culture rather than allowing hell's influence.

Takeaway

The culture of heaven doesn't happen by accident. It's built through a thousand small decisions that either honor God or give the enemy access to our lives. Start by walking in step with the Holy Spirit, allowing the fruits of the Spirit to characterize your relationships and your home. These aren't qualities you manufacture through willpower but the natural result of being filled with God's presence.

You may not influence millions, but you absolutely can influence your home. Every person who enters your space should leave feeling blessed, carrying some of that aroma of heaven with them. This is how we confront evil in our time, not just by opposing darkness but by building something so full of light that darkness cannot remain.

A Closing Prayer

Heavenly Father, help me create beauty and order in my life and identify and root out the strongholds that draw me into sin, and forgive me my transgressions. Let me be an example to others of transformation. Take away my shame, help me become a healthier person, and draw me closer to You. I want to be a disciple of Christ, obedient and steadfast in my resolve. Help me discern what lead me into sin, and guide me to find true, lasting joy in You. Amen.

Chapter 23
The Historical Jesus

In every generation, there's a temptation to remake Jesus in our own image. We take the real Christ revealed in Scripture and subtly reshape him to fit our preferences, our politics, our cultural moment. Sometimes this happens through outright deception by those who reject biblical authority. But more often, it comes from sincere believers who simply emphasize certain aspects of Jesus's character while downplaying others. Over time, these small distortions accumulate until we're left with what scholars' call "the historical Jesus," a reconstructed version that bears his name but lacks his true nature.

C. S. Lewis understood this danger well. In Letter 23, Screwtape reveals one of the more sophisticated attacks in the demonic arsenal. When obvious temptations fail to derail a mature believer, the demonic realm shifts tactics. Rather than trying to pull someone away from Christ entirely, they work to corrupt the faith from within. They redirect spiritual passion into intellectual pride, transforming genuine seekers into sophisticated scholars who study Jesus without truly knowing him. This chapter explores how this trap works, why it's so effective, and how we can return to the true Christ revealed in Scripture.

Scripture

"For if someone comes and proclaims another Jesus than the one we proclaimed, or if you receive a different spirit from the one you received, or if you accept a different gospel from the one you accepted, you put up with it readily enough."
- 2 Corinthians 11:4

The Intellectual Trap

The patient in Lewis's letter has reached a level of spiritual maturity that makes him nearly immune to obvious sins. He's walking faithfully with the Lord, attending church consistently, dating a godly woman, and surrounded by good friends who share his faith. As Christians mature in their faith and walk, this progression is natural. They grow beyond the basics, and Satan must adapt his strategy accordingly.

This presents a problem for Screwtape, who can no longer rely on common temptations to derail the man's spiritual progress. The world has failed to pull him away. The flesh has failed to pull him away. So, the demonic realm has no choice but to try corrupting him at a higher level. They work to redirect his passion for Christ, not by making him abandon Jesus, but by getting him caught up in ideas and interpretations that gradually lead him off course.

Here's how the trap works. As this man studies Scripture and encounters different theological perspectives, he begins to overemphasize certain aspects of Jesus while de-emphasizing others. Maybe he reads an academic paper that offers a fresh take on the Gospels. Maybe he hears a sermon that focuses heavily on one dimension of Christ's character. Maybe he encounters ideas from the broader culture that seem to resonate with parts of Jesus's teaching.

Over time, these influences accumulate. What starts as genuine curiosity and a desire to grow deeper can end up creating a version of Jesus that doesn't fully match Scripture.

The bait in this trap is intellectual pride. There's something deeply appealing about being part of sophisticated conversations, about having insights that go beyond what "simple believers" understand. Christians walking in good faith try to consider these new ideas. They want to be thoughtful and nuanced. But to keep up with the discussion, they feel pressure to demonstrate that they're intellectually capable of engaging at that level. They feel tempted to rise to the occasion, to show they can grasp these complex theories and contribute their own insights. Knowledge puffs up, as Paul warns. And when we start approaching Jesus primarily as an intellectual puzzle to solve rather than as our Lord and Savior to worship, we've already begun to lose our way.

This is where we need to remember something crucial. Growing in your faith doesn't mean challenging the fundamentals. Sometimes we feel like we need to discover something profound, to sound smart, to have a fresh perspective. But maturity in Christ doesn't mean relaying the foundation. The essentials don't change. Jesus is who Scripture says he is. The temptation is to think that deeper understanding requires deconstructing and reconstructing basic truths when what we really need is to know the true Christ more intimately.

Here's a story that illustrates how this works. A group of researchers (Helen Pluckrose, James A. Lindsay, and Peter Boghossian) decided to expose how easily academia could be fooled by impressive-sounding theories. They wrote a completely fake study claiming they had observed rape culture and power dynamics among dogs at urban dog parks. The paper analyzed how dogs sniffing each other and establishing dominance hierarchies supposedly reflected toxic masculinity and heteronormative oppression in human society.

Every word was invented. There were no observations, no data, no real methodology. They submitted this elaborate hoax to a prestigious peer-reviewed journal.

The reviewers gave it glowing praise, calling it "incredibly innovative, rich in analysis, and extremely well-written and organized." The paper was not only accepted for publication but was honored as leading scholarship. Peer reviewers praised its theoretical complexity and recommended it as an important contribution to feminist geography. The paper won recognition specifically because it challenged conventional thinking and offered a fresh perspective that deconstructed traditional understanding.

What made this hoax so successful wasn't just clever writing or academic jargon. The researchers knew exactly what mainstream academia was looking for. They knew that academics value brilliant new theories that rewrite the script and challenge the status quo. The reviewers were so intoxicated by the prospect of discovering something revolutionary that they completely lost sight of common sense and basic truth.

The very qualities that made the dog park paper appealing to academic reviewers are the same qualities that make false theories about Jesus attractive to Christian intellectuals who pride themselves on their sophisticated understanding. When we hear these theories and they sound intellectual, we're tempted to rise to the occasion. We want to show that we understand them, that we can engage at that level. There's an appeal to non-conformity, to challenging the status quo, to being seen as someone who has fresh insights. We might even feel zealous about these new perspectives. But ultimately, we're finding satisfaction not in truth but in appearing brilliant.

The enemy doesn't need to make us abandon scholarship entirely. He simply needs to make us value brilliant theories more than simple truth. He exploits our desire to be seen as thoughtful, nuanced, and intellectually sophisticated. Satan himself is the ultimate critic. He saw God being worshiped and criticized it. He wanted to rewrite the script of heaven itself. That same critical spirit works in us when we approach truth not to understand and submit to it, but to deconstruct and remake it in our own image.

Creating Historical Jesuses

Lewis identifies the specific pattern this intellectual corruption follows. The demonic strategy is to get people to create different versions of Jesus by suppressing certain aspects of his character and teaching while exaggerating others. Then they call this reconstructed Jesus "brilliant" or "fresh" or "what Jesus really meant all along."

This is how Jesus gets dethroned. Each one of these attempts, whether intentional or not by the humans involved, serves the devil's purpose of dethroning Christ. These reconstructed versions replace the real Jesus with one that's more convenient, more politically useful, or easier to fit into our existing worldview. Often these historical Jesuses serve an individual, a group, a generation, a culture, or even a nation. They suit particular political, social, or personal interests better than the Jesus of Scripture.

Let's unpack some of the most common versions you'll encounter in our time. Watch for the pattern in each one. Something true about Jesus gets emphasized. Something equally true about Jesus gets suppressed or ignored. The result is a Jesus who doesn't exist.

The Good Teacher Jesus

Academics treat Jesus as solely a historical figure, analyzing his life while dismissing his miracles, resurrection, and divinity. This version says he was a wise moral teacher who talked about love and helping the poor, but it strips away everything that makes him God.

The Prosperity Gospel Jesus

This version emphasizes Jesus's miraculous provision as a God who exists primarily to make you healthy, wealthy, and successful. It suppresses his warnings about wealth, his call to take up our cross, his promise of hard times for his followers, and his teaching that we store up treasures in heaven rather than on earth.

The Liberation Jesus

Liberation theology emerged during the 1960s with figures like Gustavo Gutiérrez. This version views Jesus primarily as a revolutionary who sided with the poor and oppressed, overemphasizing liberation from our circumstances while de-emphasizing liberation from sin.

The Pacifist Jesus

Peace movements emphasize Jesus's teachings like "Blessed are the peacemakers," highlighting calls to non-violence and turning the other cheek. They suppress his role as final judge, his harsh rebukes of religious hypocrisy, and the fact that he's coming back to fight with a sword.

The Pro-Choice Jesus

This version emphasizes Jesus's compassion for women and marginalized groups. It suppresses his clear affirmation of the sanctity of life, God's role as creator of life, and his consistent teaching about protecting the vulnerable.

The LGBTQ+ Jesus

This Jesus highlights acceptance of outcasts, opposition to legalistic religious leaders, and teachings on love and inclusion. It reinterprets or dismisses his clear affirmation of God's design for marriage between one man and one woman. The result validates every lifestyle choice rather than calling people to transformation.

The 'He Gets Us' Jesus

You may recall a recent Super Bowl commercial promoting this version. It attempts to make Jesus relatable by emphasizing that he understands our struggles and relates to us in our current condition. This inverts the proper relationship, reducing Christ from Savior who transforms us into a sympathetic friend who merely exists to validate and affirm us.

The Communist Jesus

This version emphasizes the early church sharing possessions, Jesus's warnings about wealth, and his concern for the poor. It suppresses his affirmation of private property, his teaching about faithful stewardship, his rebuke of laziness, and the voluntary nature of Christian generosity. The result is a Jesus who endorses state control of resources and forced redistribution.

The Woke Jesus

This Jesus focuses exclusively on his acceptance of outcasts, his challenge to power structures, and his concern for marginalized groups. It suppresses his clear moral teachings, his call to repentance, his affirmation of traditional family, and his teaching that truth exists and matters. The result is a Jesus who validates contemporary progressive ideology while ignoring most of what he actually said and did.

The Self-Help Jesus

This Jesus focuses on his teachings about abundant life and overcoming obstacles. It suppresses the gospel of sin and redemption, reducing Jesus to a life coach who helps you achieve your potential and reach your goals. Christianity becomes a program for personal development rather than reconciliation with God through the cross.

The Nationalist Jesus

This Jesus gets wrapped in a particular nation's flag and presented as endorsing that country's interests above all others. It suppresses his teaching that his kingdom is not of this world, that believers from every nation are one body, and that our ultimate allegiance belongs to him alone rather than to any earthly government.

The "Bro" Jesus

This casual, approachable Jesus emphasizes his friendship with disciples and sinners. It suppresses his holiness, his righteous anger, his role as judge, and the reverent fear appropriate when approaching the Creator of the universe. The result is a Jesus who's more like your easygoing friend than the King of kings and Lord of lords.

The Religious Jesus

Some emphasize Jesus's moral teachings, his calls to holiness, and his warnings about judgment. They suppress his grace toward sinners, his mercy toward the broken, his criticism of legalism, and his offer of rest for the weary. This creates a harsh taskmaster Jesus who piles on rules but offers no hope or help to those who fail.

Each of these approaches takes genuine aspects of Jesus's character and ministry but distorts them by removing them from their proper biblical context. The pattern is always the same. Suppress one aspect of Christ's character. Exaggerate another. Call the result "brilliant" or "what Jesus really meant." And suddenly you have a Jesus who fits comfortably within your framework but bears little resemblance to the Christ revealed in Scripture. If we're not careful, even faithful believers fall into this trap. That's exactly what Screwtape knew. That's what he was counting on with the patient. It's a sober warning for all of us.

Returning to the True Jesus

Here we arrive at perhaps the most significant observation Lewis makes in this entire letter. This is one of the very few places in all of Lewis's writings where he explicitly and directly mentions the resurrection of Jesus Christ. Even the demons, Lewis suggests, understand that this historical reality is what truly matters. All the brilliant theories, all the sophisticated analyses, all the clever reconstructions pale in comparison to this simple fact. Jesus died and rose again.

Paul makes this abundantly clear. "For I delivered to you as of first importance what I also received, that Christ died for our sins in accordance with the Scriptures, that he was buried, that he was raised on the third day in accordance with the Scriptures" (1 Corinthians 15:3-4). This is the gospel. Everything else, as important as it might be, is built on this foundation.

The resurrection validates everything else we believe about Jesus. It confirms his divine nature, his victory over death and Satan, and his promise of eternal life for those who trust in him. When we lose sight of this central reality, we reduce Christianity to just another human ideology. The resurrection is what makes Jesus unique among all the historical figures who have ever lived.

As you grow in faith and explore deeper theological waters, you might accidentally overemphasize one aspect of Jesus's character while underemphasizing another. Keep pursuing truth with humility and extend grace to yourself and others. The key is remaining teachable and willing to adjust your understanding when it conflicts with Scripture.

The solution to the intellectual trap is not rejecting scholarship. God gave us minds to use for his glory. The problem arises when scholarship becomes an end in itself rather than a means to know God better. True spiritual maturity is marked not by the complexity of our theological theories but by the depth of our love for Christ and our conformity to his character.

Jesus is both lion and lamb. He's the one who came in gentleness to die for our sins, and he's the one coming back with a sword, riding on a white horse, with eyes like blazing fire. The goal of all Christian learning should be to know this Jesus better and become more like him, not to develop brilliant insights that make us look sophisticated. When scholarship stops leading us to worship and starts making us proud of our insights, we've lost our way.

Takeaway

The intellectual trap reveals how even good desires can become spiritual dangers when divorced from humble worship. The desire to understand Jesus better is good. Theological study is valuable. But when scholarship becomes an end in itself, when we value brilliant theories more than simple truth, when we're more concerned with sounding sophisticated than with knowing Christ, we've been ensnared. The antidote is keeping the main thing the main thing. Jesus died for your sins. He was buried. He rose again. He conquered death. He's coming back. Everything else is built on this foundation.

A Closing Prayer

Dear Jesus, I want to understand you more, meet with me as I read my Bible, and pour into me that I may be filled with your Word. Let me be guided by the Spirit that I will not make a version of you that fits my needs but help me create a version of me that fits your calling. Guard me from the sin of pride and give me discernment to see through the lies of the enemy. In the name of the true resurrected Lord, Amen.

Chapter 24
Haughty Eyes and Spiritual Pride

Spiritual maturity is a journey that requires constant dedication. As we grow, new challenges emerge that require us to examine every aspect of our walk with Christ. The temptations we face as mature believers look different from those we encountered as new Christians. One of the most insidious is spiritual pride. It creeps in quietly when we're surrounded by godly people, growing in knowledge, and making real progress. It manifests as a subtle shift in how we view others who aren't part of our circle, whether they're believers from different stripes or those who don't yet know Christ.

This chapter addresses how the very communities meant to sharpen us can become exclusive groups that isolate us from the world we're called to reach.

Scripture

"There are six things the LORD hates, seven that are an abomination to him: haughty eyes, a lying tongue, and hands that shed innocent blood, a heart that devises wicked plans, feet that make haste to run to evil, a false witness who breathes out lies, and one who sows discord among brothers."
- Proverbs 6:16-19

The Chink in the Armor

As we've referenced in recent chapters, we find in Letter 24 that the patient is surrounded by good influences. He has a faithful Christian girlfriend from a strong family, he's part of a healthy church community, and he's growing spiritually. When Satan's typical attacks aren't working, his strategy shifts to something more sophisticated.

Lewis introduces another demon, Slumtrimpet, who is in charge of the patient's girlfriend. This shows us how demons collaborate and reveals a vulnerability in her spiritual armor. Screwtape discovers the chink he's been looking for. The girlfriend has what Lewis describes as an ignorant naivety. She assumes that people who don't share her beliefs are too stupid or ridiculous to understand the faith. But this isn't malicious pride. It's sheltered ignorance from a good upbringing. She's only ever known Christianity, surrounded by comfort, intellectual sophistication, and godly character. It seems like faith has always made sense because everyone around her believed it and lived it well.

Here's the demonic strategy. Get the patient to imitate this small flaw of haughtiness and exaggerate it until it becomes full-blown spiritual pride. What starts as a subtle, haughty outlook can turn into a debilitating character flaw. The conditions are ideal. He's now part of what Lewis calls a better educated, more intelligent, more agreeable society than he's ever encountered. The danger is that he'll think he belongs there by right, rather than recognizing he's been graciously received. He'll feel the sweet appeal of the inner ring, of being one of the select few in a sophisticated Christian circle. Even the healthiest Christian home doesn't make you exempt from sin. You cannot coast on the faith of those around you. You must cling to Christ yourself, work out your own salvation, and remain humble before God. No one is exempt from this struggle.

When Community Becomes Clique

Believers often begin adopting the culture of their Christian community without truly wrestling with it themselves. They echo their pastor's theological positions, adopt their friends' views on Scripture, and start correcting others on doctrines they couldn't have explained months ago. It can become an echo chamber. One person reads a book or commentary, then everyone else in the group reads it, and they all validate each other's conclusions. The group develops shared language, shared convictions, and shared opinions. And this isn't limited to young believers. Even established Christians fall into this pattern.

The problem is that discipleship gets confused with tribalism. Believers can point to memorized verses, books they've read, and active participation in small groups. But underneath, they've merely joined a tribe. Their identity rests on knowing the right answers and belonging to the right crowd, not on being transformed by Christ. You cannot piggyback on another person's faith. You cannot borrow their convictions. You will stand before the Lord to give an account for what you believed and why. While it's good to learn from spiritual leaders and sit under sound teaching, if you haven't wrestled with Scripture yourself through personal study and prayer, you haven't grown. You've just joined a club.

This breeds a Pharisaical spirit that manifests in two ways. First, looking down on other believers. You start viewing Christians from other denominations as people who don't do church the right way. They lack the theological precision you've acquired. They emphasize the wrong things or hold inferior positions. You make secondary issues into litmus tests for who's truly walking with God. Whether Christians practice infant baptism or believer's baptism, sing hymns or contemporary songs, take communion with wine or grape juice, these are matters of Christian freedom. If someone believes in the deity of Christ, the authority of Scripture, salvation by grace through faith, and the call to make disciples, they're your brother or sister in Christ.

Second, looking down on nonbelievers. We can view non-Christians as too ignorant, too uneducated, or too sinful to grasp your faith. Former friends who aren't believers seem like foolish people who didn't make it into the nice club you've joined. This is where crossing the wires happens. It's wise to establish boundaries with people who pull you toward sin. Proverbs warns against keeping company with fools. If you have friends encouraging you away from Christ, you need distance. But Satan twists that good principle. Once you've established healthy boundaries and surrounded yourself with godly friends, he tempts you to take it too far. Now everyone outside your Christian circle becomes someone to avoid. Before you know it, you've gone from wise boundaries to an isolated fortress. God wants you to build connections with people who need to hear the gospel. But Satan wants to use your spiritual maturity as an excuse to keep you away from the very people who most need to see Christ in you.

God Closes Gaps, Satan Creates Them

Here's a helpful way of thinking about this issue. God is always trying to close gaps, and Satan is always trying to create them. Think about the biblical narrative. In the Garden, sin entered and immediately created a gap between God and humanity. Separation, distance, alienation. From that moment forward, the story of Scripture is God working to close that gap. He makes covenants, gives the Law, sends prophets, and ultimately sends His own Son to bridge the chasm that sin created.

Jesus Christ is the ultimate gap closer. Philippians 2:16 tells us that although He existed in the form of God, He didn't consider equality with God something to be grasped. Instead, He emptied Himself, taking on the form of a servant, being born in the likeness of men. He humbled Himself to the point of death on a cross. Why? To close the gap and make a way for humanity to be reconciled to God.

Satan's strategy is the opposite. He works to create distance and division. He separates believers from God through sin, tears families apart, and divides churches over secondary issues. When he can't corrupt a faithful Christian surrounded by a godly community, he shifts tactics. He fosters spiritual pride to isolate them. He builds walls between them and the world they're called to reach. He turns someone who was meant to be salt and light into an ineffective, self-righteous figure in an ivory tower, viewing non-Christians as too ignorant or sinful to bother with. This is exactly what's happening with the young believer in Lewis's letter, and it renders him useless to the kingdom.

Confessions of a Pompous Bible Student

I've seen this dynamic in my own life and looking back. I grew up in a Baptist church and attended a Baptist university. I'm deeply grateful for my background. The churches I grew up in had a high regard for Scripture and taught me to study the Bible carefully. But one weakness I observed was a tendency toward insularity. If you weren't doing church the Baptist way, there was often an unspoken (and sometimes spoken) assumption that you were doing it wrong.

During my college years, I was part of a church with two distinct groups. Bible college students and state university students. The Bible college students, myself included, carried a certain attitude. We were studying theology, parsing Greek verbs, being trained for ministry. Looking back, we had a sense of superiority over the state university students. We never said it out loud, but it was there.

There was one guy named Josh who was part of the state university group. Josh had come to faith later in life and didn't have a theological education. He was involved in various campus ministries and attended churches outside our tradition. If I'm honest, I looked at Josh with haughtiness. I appreciated his passion, but there was this unspoken assumption that I was further along, more doctrinally sound, better positioned for ministry.

Years later, I reconnected with Josh and discovered he had faithfully pursued ministry. He had served as a youth pastor, then associate pastor, and eventually became a senior pastor. He had a beautiful family, a thriving church, and a genuine heart for Jesus. I felt convicted. Here I had been, so proud of my education, and Josh had simply been faithful. I reached out and apologized for any superiority I might have communicated. Thankfully, Josh received my apology graciously.

That experience taught me something crucial. The Lord detests haughty eyes. All my theological training, all my Bible college experience, all my knowledge meant nothing if it produced pride instead of humility. Josh's steady faithfulness in ministry was worth far more than my supposed sophistication.

The Humility of Christ, The Call to Be Salt and Light

If we're going to combat spiritual pride, we need to remember something foundational. We didn't earn our place in the Christian community. We were welcomed in. We didn't deserve God's love and salvation. It was freely given. We're standing on ground we didn't prepare and drinking from wells we didn't dig. When the patient in

Lewis's letter was first brought into his girlfriend's family and church, he was the recipient of grace. People invested in him, taught him, embraced him. But he's forgotten that. He now sees himself as someone who belongs there by right. This is the soil in which haughtiness grows.

The antidote is looking at the humility of Christ. The same passage we used earlier to illustrate God closing the gap is one of the primary passages in Scripture to explain Christ's humility and service toward others. Consider the gap between Jesus and humanity. We talk about differences between educated Christians and uneducated nonbelievers, between mature believers and immature seekers. But all those gaps are microscopic compared to the chasm between God and man. Jesus is infinite in wisdom, perfect in holiness, the Creator of all things. If anyone had the right to look down on humanity, it was Him. Yet He didn't respond with contempt. He responded by closing the gap. Remember Philippians 2 again, it tells us the story of His humility and then says, "Have this mind among yourselves, which is yours in Christ Jesus" (Phil. 2:5). He took on flesh, entered our world, lived among us, ate with sinners, touched lepers, engaged with prostitutes and tax collectors. He humbled Himself to the point of death on a cross to make a way for reconciliation. This is the attitude we're called to have. If Christ could bridge the infinite gap between divinity and humanity, how can we justify creating distance over trivial differences?

When spiritual pride takes hold, we forget we're meant to be salt and light in the world. Jesus didn't call us to be salt and light primarily in a church building, but to a lost and dying world. Both images assume we're in contact with the world. You can't be salt locked in a shaker or light hidden under a basket. Yet that's exactly what spiritual pride does. It isolates Christians in holy huddles where they're safe but ineffective. Consider your own story. There was a time when you didn't know Christ, when you were far from God, walking in darkness. Someone extended grace to you. Someone shared the gospel with you. Someone was patient with your questions. Are you now extending that same grace to others?

Takeaway

The key to combating spiritual pride is remembering you are a perpetual recipient of grace. You didn't earn your place. You were welcomed. Every blessing, every bit of spiritual growth, every insight into Scripture came from God's kindness and the investment of others who poured into your life.

When you remember you're standing on ground you didn't prepare and drinking from wells you didn't dig, it transforms how you look at others. Instead of viewing non-Christians with contempt, you see them as people who need the same grace you received. Check your spiritual pride at the door. The Lord detests haughty eyes. Our calling is to extend to others the grace that was so freely given to us.

A Closing Prayer

Dear Lord, forgive me for my haughty eyes and the pride that led me to believe I was more worthy than others. Help me move forward with a humble heart and a generous spirit, praising You all the days of my life. Give me discernment to walk in truth and reach out to those in need, not with pride or judgment, but with compassion and grace. Let me be salt and light in this world, reflecting Your goodness in all I do. For You are good and Your mercies are endless. In Christ's name, Amen.

Chapter 25
The Horror of the Same Old Thing

In Letter 25, C. S. Lewis introduces a phrase that would become central to another of his crucial works. He describes the patient and his circle of Christian friends as being satisfied with "mere Christianity." Mere Christianity is Christianity at its core, undiluted and unadulterated. Pure faith in Jesus Christ without the additions, modifications, or trendy attachments that every generation tries to impose.

Lewis understood something fundamental about human nature and spiritual warfare. We have a natural craving for novelty, a "horror of the same old thing." And Satan exploits this desire brilliantly. He takes our legitimate longing for growth and progress and twists it into a pursuit of fashionable causes and trendy additions to the gospel. This is personal for every believer. We all feel the pull to make our faith relevant, to align with the cultural moment, to show we're not stuck in the past. But before we know it, we're no longer practicing Christianity. We're practicing Christianity plus something else. And that addition, no matter how noble it may seem, ends up displacing Christ from the center of our faith.

Scripture

"Jesus Christ is the same yesterday, today, and forever. Do not be carried about with various and strange doctrines." - Hebrews 13:8-9 (NKJV)

The Horror of the Same Old Thing

God designed human beings with a paradox built into our nature. Lewis describes it well. We desire both change and permanence. We crave variety but also need stability. Think about the rhythms of creation. God gave us seasons that cycle through the year, bringing change and variety, yet returning with reliable permanence. There's change within constancy, variety within stability. This is beautiful design. The same pattern plays out in our lives. We establish routines and rhythms. We get married and create stable homes. We pick a church and attend regularly. We celebrate the same holidays every year. There's constancy that anchors us. But within that framework, we fill our days with variety. We pursue hobbies, try new restaurants, and read different books. We need both change and permanence.

This is how God wired us, and it's good. The problem comes when Satan takes this natural desire and perverts it. He makes us feel like we're stagnating if we're not constantly chasing something new. He exploits our fear that maybe we're stuck, maybe we're not progressing, maybe we're falling behind or missing out on the next big thing. And once he's instilled that fear, he's ready with a solution. Add something to your faith. Update it. Make it relevant. Bring in the new cause, the trendy ideology, the fashionable movement.

This is where a subtle shift happens. When we feel spiritually restless or discontented, we start looking for ways to spice things up.

We think we need to add something to make our faith feel fresh, exciting, or culturally engaged. Maybe it's a social movement that promises justice. Maybe it's a cause that feels urgent. Maybe it's a theological emphasis that sounds sophisticated. Maybe it's even something good like fitness or family or career success that becomes so central it crowds out Christ. Whatever it is, we start building our identity around Christianity plus something else.

The gospel is complete. The gospel is sufficient. When we start adding things to Christianity, we make it Christianity plus social movements, Christianity plus our political party, Christianity plus any cause or ideology, we're not enhancing the faith. We're diluting it. We're distorting it. We're displacing Christ from the center.

Our pastor often would say a phrase worth remembering, "Jesus plus anything ruins everything."

Here's the right way to think about it. Your life should be like a cup filled to overflowing with Jesus. When your cup is full of your relationship with the Lord, when you're saturated with Scripture and walking in the Spirit and letting Christ transform you from the inside out, then your faith overflows into every area of your life. It pours into your politics, your social views, your work, your family, your hobbies, your friendships. Everything you do becomes an expression of your faith because Jesus is at the center and He's overflowing into everything else.

But that's not what's happening in much of the modern church today. Instead, people are filling their cups with causes, movements, and cultural priorities, and then they're trying to add Jesus to it. They're starting with their politics and looking for Bible verses to support it. They're starting with their social agenda and trying to retrofit Christianity to accommodate it. That's backwards. That's the cup being filled from the outside rather than overflowing from the inside. And it results in a faith that's not "mere" Christianity anymore. It's something else with a Christian label slapped on it.

"Christianity Plus" in Our Time

There are certain moments and issues that reveal whether Jesus is actually at the center of our faith or if He's been pushed to the periphery to make room for something else. These are litmus tests. These are dividing lines that expose what we truly value and what we've allowed to displace Christ.

One underlying issue corrupting much of the modern church today is rooted in what's called critical theory. Critical theory is an approach that takes something established and systematically deconstructs it. It criticizes every aspect, questions every foundation, and seeks to tear down what has been built. This is the intellectual framework behind so much of what we're seeing in our cultural moment, and it's directly tied to the horror of the same old thing. Satan amplifies our fear of stagnation and then offers critical theory as the solution. Don't just accept what's been handed down. Challenge it. Deconstruct it. Rebuild it according to the values of this current generation and fresh new insights.

Satan himself operates as a critic. Scripture calls him "the accuser." That critical spirit is at work in the modern church, convincing believers that the old ways are outdated, that traditional biblical teaching needs to be reexamined. It starts with identifying perceived problems, some of which may be real. But instead of reforming from within the biblical framework, it deconstructs everything. And that deconstruction leads to places the church was never meant to go.

So, what does critical theory add to Christianity? What becomes the "plus" in Christianity Plus? Let's look at a few.

We see it in the sexual revolution and LGBT+ ideology. Churches are flying rainbow flags, rewriting biblical sexuality, redefining marriage, and gutting Scripture to accommodate their preferred sexual belief systems. Some denominations are more concerned with affirming gender ideology than proclaiming the gospel. This is Christianity plus a new enlightened perspective on sexuality and gender. They've deconstructed God's design for sex, marriage, and gender, and rebuilt it according to cultural demands. It's the fruit of a critical spirit that couldn't rest content with the faith once delivered to the saints. And it's being done in the name of love, inclusion, and justice, all while claiming to follow Jesus.

We also see it in movements like Black Lives Matter. The 2020 BLM riots were not expressions of biblical justice. They were social insurrections founded on critical race theory, a worldview that redefines truth and righteousness to fit a narrative. Many churches jumped on board, not because Scripture led them there, but because cultural pressure demanded it. This was Christianity plus a new form of justice. They had deconstructed traditional understandings of justice, law and order, and personal responsibility, and replaced them with a system that prioritizes group identity and perceived systemic oppression.

Feminism and the attack on the traditional family are other striking examples of these distortions in our day. Critical theory has targeted God's design for men and women, marriage, and family. The assault on masculinity, the redefinition of gender roles, and the diminishing of fatherhood are all fruits of deconstructionist thinking. This is Christianity plus liberation from so-called patriarchal structures. Churches that embrace this have dismantled biblical manhood and womanhood, and rebuilt family according to secular feminist ideals.

Let us be clear. This is not Christianity. This is Christianity Plus taken to its logical conclusion, where the "plus" has overtaken everything else. This is what happens when ideology displaces Christ from the center. These aren't churches where people's faith is overflowing into their engagement with culture. These are examples where demonic ideas have influenced the church and corrupted it from the inside out.

But Christianity Plus doesn't only manifest through critical theory. Sometimes it appears as acquiescence to cultural pressures and priorities that seem less radical but are just as dangerous.

The COVID-19 church closures revealed which pastors understood the priority of worship and which ones had elevated something else above it. Strip clubs and liquor stores remained open, petitioning the courts and waving the First Amendment. Yet churches were chained shut, deemed too dangerous for worship. What had many churches added to their faith? Government approval. Public perception. An inflated sense of health and safety that displaced their confidence in God's sovereignty. They practiced Christianity plus compliance with the state. When the government said gathering for worship was non-essential, they agreed. They had allowed cultural priorities around safety and being seen as responsible citizens to override their biblical conviction that the gathered church is essential. That was Christianity Plus in its most visible form.

We also need to address errors on the other side of the political and social spectrum. One of the most serious tendencies we see today is toward Christian nationalism. Christian nationalism is Christianity plus nationalism. Now, let me be clear. We are called to be Christians, and we can be patriots. We can love our country. But Christian nationalism conflates the two in an unhealthy way. It's the misguided application of Christian theology in the political realm, specifically trying to institute Christianity as a mandated state religion.

Here's the crucial distinction. "Christianity" and "nationalism" can inform each other, but they should not define each other. Your faith should inform your civic engagement. Your biblical values should shape how you vote, what policies you support, and how you understand justice and human flourishing. That's appropriate. That's faith overflowing into your citizenship. But when nationalism becomes so intertwined with your faith that you can't distinguish between allegiance to country and allegiance to Christ, you've crossed into Christianity Plus territory. When you start believing that the government should enforce Christian doctrine, ordain pastors, or take theological positions, you've made nationalism part of your gospel. This leads to the government running the church. That's dangerous and wrong.

It is a fine balance. To paraphrase Paul in Romans 31:1, we submit to authority inasmuch as we do not disobey God. What we are called to do is allow our Christian values to inform our engagement in the public square. As we've discussed in this book, we are to be salt and light. We are to speak truth with clarity and conviction. We are to vote according to our biblical values, not according to what's popular or convenient. We are to advocate for policies that protect life, preserve religious liberty, uphold biblical sexuality, defend the vulnerable, and promote human flourishing as God defines it. We are to walk in our full authority as members of society, as image-bearers of God with inalienable rights and civic duties.

We're not trying to use government to force people to become Christians. We're trying to live as Christians in a free society and to shape that society toward righteousness as much as we're able. The difference is subtle but crucial. One flows from Christ at the center.

The other puts political power at the center and tries to baptize it with Christian language. Both the left and the right can fall into the trap of Christianity Plus. We must be vigilant on all sides.

Innovating Without Changing the Core

So how do we walk this out practically? How do we pursue growth, cultural engagement, and avoid stagnation without falling into the trap of Christianity Plus?

Understand that churches can and should innovate in methods without changing the message. We should be looking for new and better ways to integrate our faith into society. We should be exploring alternative approaches to education, considering how public schools often work against biblical values. We should be thinking creatively about how to engage the university system, how to reach the next generation. We should be studying theology more, engaging with the open-handed disagreements between denominations, and growing in our understanding of Scripture.

What can become problematic is when we start innovating in doctrine itself. When we start updating theology to be more palatable and less convicting to modern sensibilities, when we rewrite Scripture to align with cultural trends, that's when we've crossed the line into corruption. The core tenets of Christianity don't change. Jesus lived, died, rose again, and ascended into heaven. That's not up for debate. Salvation is through grace alone, by faith alone, not by works, but lived out through them. That's not negotiable. The Bible is God's authoritative Word. These are foundational truths, and no amount of cultural pressure should move us to compromise them. In the world today, we feel the need to add God's design for sexuality, marriage, and gender to this list. Churches that abandon these truths in the name of relevance aren't being innovative. They're being apostate.

Also remember that true change comes through sanctification, not through chasing trendy causes. Sanctification is the slow process by which God conforms you to the image of Christ. It's the work of the Holy Spirit transforming your character, renewing your mind, purifying your desires, and making you more like Jesus day by day. This is a slow work. Sometimes it feels like the same old thing. But that's the change we should be pursuing. That's the growth we should be after.

Here's a crucial warning. When nonconformity becomes your identity, you've perverted Christianity. If your sense of self is wrapped up in being a rebel and challenging the status quo, if you're driven by fear of the same old thing rather than by faithfulness to Christ, you've fallen into the trap. Your pursuit of novelty has displaced your pursuit of holiness.

Takeaway

We must be wise as serpents and gentle as doves. There is a natural pull from our hearts to engage with culture, to address the issues of our day. The tension is real. We can be involved in the wrong ways or not involved enough in the right ways. We need discernment. Times change. Culture shifts. We must discern the times well. But we must not be pulled or led by the horror of the same old thing.

Resist the temptation of Christianity Plus. The moment you add something to Jesus; you've diluted the gospel. Let your faith overflow from a heart filled with Christ into every area of your life. But nothing should displace Jesus from the center. The change you should be pursuing is not the novelty of fashionable causes. It's sanctification. It's being conformed to the image of Christ through the work of the Holy Spirit, day by day, year by year. That's the growth that matters. Keep Jesus at the center. Let Him overflow into everything else. And resist every demonic attempt to get you to add anything to the simple, pure, powerful gospel of Jesus Christ.

A Closing Prayer

Heavenly Father, my God, my Lord Jesus Christ, keep my eyes fixed on You, and help me keep You at the center of my life, without distortion, without wavering. Lord, You are my constant, my rock, and my salvation. I will walk with You all the days of my life. Let me not fall for the lies and deceit of the enemy but remain firm in my faith in You. Thank You for Your Word, which guides me and helps me discern truth on this journey. Forgive me when I sin and fall short of Your glory and sanctify me by Your love and grace. In Jesus name, Amen.

Chapter 26
False Humility

Letter 26 reveals one of Satan's most subtle attacks on relationships. He doesn't tempt you toward obvious sin like cheating, lying, or neglecting your spouse. Instead, he twists something genuinely good into something quietly destructive. He takes real love and replaces it with a counterfeit version that looks holy but poisons marriages from the inside. Here's how it works. You sacrifice something for your spouse. You give up what you want and go along with their plans. But deep down, you're keeping score. You're building a mental list of everything you've surrendered. No one actually gets blessed by your sacrifice. The only result is a growing pile of resentment in your heart that will eventually poison everything.

Lewis calls this hollow imitation "unselfishness." It looks like love. It feels like you're being a good Christian. But it's empty. Real love, what the Bible calls charity, is completely different. Real love sacrifices to genuinely help the other person. Counterfeit love sacrifices to make yourself look good while setting up future resentment. When Jesus commanded us to "love your neighbor as yourself," He wasn't talking about surface-level niceness. He was calling us to genuine care that costs you something and actually blesses someone else. The question we need to answer is this. How do we love the right way? How do we avoid the trap of fake selflessness that slowly destroys our most important relationships?

Scripture

"The purpose in a man's heart is like deep water, but a man of understanding will draw it out." - Proverbs 20:5

Love's Order and The Counterfeit Version

We need to understand what we're dealing with. There's authentic love, and there's a counterfeit that Satan eagerly offers. The difference between them determines whether your marriage flourishes or slowly dies.

Real love is what the Bible calls charity. Charity means sacrificing with a specific aim to genuinely help someone. When I give up something I want, the point is that you receive something good. My sacrifice has a purpose beyond making me look noble. You're actually blessed because I gave something up. That's charity. It's focused on your good, not on proving my holiness.

The counterfeit is what Lewis calls "negative unselfishness." Here's what it looks like. You give something up, but nobody actually benefits. You just wanted credit for being selfless. You wanted to feel virtuous. You wanted to tell yourself you're a good Christian spouse. But your husband or wife didn't gain anything real from what you did. The sacrifice happened in a vacuum.

Think of it this way. In baseball, a sacrifice fly only counts if a run scores. If nobody advances, it's just an out. In marriage, a sacrifice that doesn't genuinely bless your spouse isn't love. It's just you keeping score and setting yourself up to feel cheated later.

Here's where it gets deceptive. Both versions look identical from the outside. Both involve giving something up. Both involve saying yes when you might want to say no. But the heart behind them is completely different. One leads to mutual joy and deeper connection. The other leads to quiet bitterness and eventually resentment.

Satan doesn't need to make you obviously selfish to wreck your marriage. He just needs to give you this counterfeit version of love. He needs you to believe that denying yourself is automatically godly, regardless of whether it serves anyone. He needs you to start counting everything you've surrendered. Once you start keeping that mental ledger, resentment grows like an untended weed that eventually chokes out genuine affection.

There's a proverb that speaks directly to this dynamic. "Hope deferred makes the heart sick, but a desire fulfilled is a tree of life," (Proverbs 13:12). If you constantly defer your desires in the name of unselfishness, refusing to ever name or pursue what you truly want, your heart will gradually grow sick with unspoken resentment. If you never express what brings you joy, never pursue what makes you feel alive, you're slowly hollowing yourself out from the inside.

But when desires are honestly named and sometimes fulfilled, life and vitality grow. That's the tree of life the proverb describes. Part of loving each other well is learning what each person genuinely wants and creating space for those desires to flourish within the marriage.

Seeds Planted During Dating

This problem often takes root when couples are dating. When you're falling in love, everything feels effortless. You say yes to everything. You constantly deny yourself. You call it love. But here's what's really happening. You're forming patterns. You're building relational habits. Screwtape tells Wormwood to plant seeds during courtship that will grow into bitterness a decade down the line. These unhealthy patterns will resurface years later in your marriage with devastating consequences.

During dating, the emotions are intense. You don't notice the cost of always saying yes. You don't notice that you're never expressing what you truly want. The intoxication of new love masks the problem. But feelings inevitably fade. Marriage becomes everyday life. Now you're not running on the high of new romance anymore. You're just living together, navigating bills and schedules and in-laws and all the friction of real life. And all those habits you built, all that false unselfishness, all that scorekeeping, it all comes roaring back with a vengeance.

The Bible tells us to love our neighbor as ourselves. Notice that phrase carefully. As ourselves. That assumes healthy love includes healthy self-regard. You can't love your spouse well if you completely erase yourself. You can't give what you don't have. You can't bless someone if you don't understand your own needs and desires.

Here's another instance of crossing the wires. Satan gets you to respond the wrong way at the wrong time. You deny yourself when you should speak up about your needs. You assert yourself when you should graciously yield. You lose the ability to discern the difference between healthy sacrifice and unhealthy martyrdom. Both denying yourself and expressing your needs can be godly, depending on the situation. Wisdom is knowing which one belongs when.

If you habitually give in with a sigh and a defeated tone, you're training your heart to resent your spouse. If you never give in, you're training your spouse to stop asking you for anything. Neither pattern reflects real love. Genuine charity lives in the truthful middle. Sometimes you joyfully say yes. Sometimes you honestly say no. The key is clear honest communication and maintaining a soft heart.

God's Design of Mutual Blessing

Here's how God designed marriage to work. Two people both willingly sacrifice for each other. My sacrifice is aimed at your joy. Your sacrifice is aimed at my joy. When this operates as intended, everybody wins.

Consider Christ's example. His sacrifice wasn't merely about appearing holy. His sacrifice was deliberately aimed at our good. He gave Himself up so that we would be saved. That's the model we're called to follow. Real sacrifice has a target. It's intentionally trying to accomplish something beneficial for someone else.

In a godly marriage, this creates a beautiful upward spiral. I invest my time, money, and energy to bless you. But here's what makes it work. God wired me to experience joy when you flourish. So, when my sacrifice genuinely blesses you, I gain something too. Not because you owe me anything. Not because I'm keeping a ledger. But because watching you thrive brings me genuine happiness.

When you do the same for me, marriage becomes truly win-win. We're both giving. We're both receiving. We're both blessed. That's God's brilliant design.

But here's the crucial balance. Charity doesn't mean you always have to say yes to everything. Sometimes the most loving response is to say calmly, "I can't do that tonight." The critical difference is honest communication versus quiet martyrdom. If you can't participate joyfully, it's better to be honest about it. A consistent pattern of joyful yeses and honest nos is far healthier than constant fake and fruitless yeses accompanied by a resentful heart.

Living This Out in Real Life

So how do we actually practice this? How do we love well in the midst of real life with demanding jobs, growing kids, tight budgets, packed schedules, and all the daily friction where unselfishness and genuine charity easily get confused?

It's so important to have genuine self-awareness. Proverbs teaches, "The purpose in a man's heart is like deep water, but a man of understanding will draw it out," Proverbs 20:5. Godliness isn't about completely erasing yourself or denying that you have legitimate needs and desires. It's about understanding what's truly in your heart and then choosing wisely where to sacrifice and where to pursue your own flourishing.

It's good and healthy for you to know what brings you genuine joy. What meals do you truly love? What experiences make you feel close to your spouse? How do you want to spend your birthday? What are your meaningful goals for work and life? If you can't articulate these things clearly, how can your spouse possibly love you well? They can't read your mind or intuit desires you've never expressed.

The same principle applies to your spouse. They need to know and be able to express what they authentically want. How do they envision parenting? Do they desire weekly date nights? Where would they love to vacation? What lifestyle do they imagine for your future together? If they immediately jump to "my desires don't matter because I want to be selfless," that's not actually godly. That's counterfeit humility. It's an imitation of virtue that slowly hollows a person out and prevents genuine intimacy.

Forgive freely and repent quickly when you mess up. You're absolutely going to make mistakes in this area. That's inevitable and okay. What truly poisons love isn't making occasional errors. It's stubbornly refusing to confess when you're wrong and refusing to forgive when you've been wronged. Work hard to keep your heart consistently soft and responsive.

Finally, keep the ultimate goal crystal clear in your mind. God's aim for your marriage isn't for you to become impressively skilled at denying yourself or to rack up points for personal sacrifice. His aim is love. Real, tangible, concrete blessings generously shared between two imperfect people who both belong to Him and to each other.

Sometimes it's even appropriate and healthy to be a little selfish. Express a strong preference clearly. Pursue a personal desire within reasonable bounds. Then genuinely reflect on whether you pushed too hard and repent if necessary. It's far better to be honest about what you want and adjust course if needed than to bury legitimate desires under fake unselfishness and watch them harden into stubborn bitterness over time.

Takeaway

The biblical command to "love your neighbor as yourself," (Mark 12:31) is frequently misunderstood. Notice carefully that it assumes you already know how to love yourself appropriately. It assumes you have healthy self-regard under God's authority. You simply can't love your neighbor or your spouse well if you don't understand how to care for yourself in godly ways.

Be vigilant not to mistake empty unselfishness for genuine charity. Unselfishness itself is neutral, like a universal blood donor. In God's hands, when guided by love and wisdom, it becomes truly beautiful and life-giving. In Satan's hands, when detached from love's actual aim, it becomes mere theater, exhausting scorekeeping, or stubborn resentment waiting to explode.

Authentic charity doesn't just spotlight your personal sacrifice to make you look heroic. It secures your spouse's genuine good and flourishing. In both courtship and marriage, actively refuse the counterfeit version. Draw your heart's deepest desires up from the hidden depths. Name them honestly. Share them vulnerably. Practice a sustainable rhythm of joyful giving and honest receiving. Love your neighbor as yourself, which necessarily means you must first understand how to love yourself well under God's wise and loving authority.

A Closing Prayer

Dear Lord, teach me to love with genuine charity, not counterfeit unselfishness that only breeds resentment. Help me truly understand my own heart so I can love others authentically and well. Give me the courage to honestly name my desires and the wisdom to discern when to sacrifice and when to speak up about my needs. Let me love my spouse the way You love me, with sacrifice that truly blesses and joy that genuinely gives without keeping score. Keep my heart soft and responsive. Help me forgive freely and repent quickly when I fail. Make my relationships a living picture of Your selfless love for us. In Jesus' name, Amen.

Chapter 27
Persistent Prayer

Prayer is one of God's greatest gifts to His children, yet it often feels like one of the hardest disciplines to maintain. Our minds wander. We struggle to articulate what we truly need. We question whether our prayers actually accomplish anything. These struggles are universal, and they're exactly what the enemy exploits to neutralize our prayer lives. Prayer, at its core, is an emotional and relational act, not merely an intellectual one. Yes, we use our minds and articulate requests. But the fuel of prayer is the heart's cry. We can pray without perfect understanding or eloquent words. We can pray when our minds wander and our thoughts scatter. God receives it all because prayer is about relationship, not performance.

In Letter 27, Screwtape reveals a surprising frustration. The patient's mind keeps wandering during prayer, distracted by romance and the anxieties of war. This should be a demonic victory. But the man keeps praying anyway, and more troubling still, his very distraction has become the subject of his prayers, "Lord, I can't focus. My mind keeps wandering. Help me." By bringing his struggle to God in simple honesty, he's stumbled into something powerful that frustrates hell itself. Prayer offered in humble faith, even stumbling and inarticulate prayer, accomplishes more in the unseen realm than eloquent words spoken without genuine trust in God.

Scripture

"Let us then approach God's throne of grace with confidence, so that we may receive mercy and find grace to help us in our time of need." - Hebrews 4:16

Praying When You Can't Find the Words

Prayer is not necessarily an intellectual exercise. It's the cry of a child to a Father. It's the pouring out of a heart that needs help, comfort, or simply the presence of someone who understands. When we reduce prayer to something we must perform correctly with the right words and proper theological framing, we miss what God invites us into. He wants our honesty more than our eloquence. He wants our hearts more than our polished presentations.

Wormwood's patient grasps this instinctively. His mind wanders and his prayers lack discipline, yet he brings that very failure to God. This is prayer in its most potent form, stripped of pretense and performance, offered in raw faith that God hears.

Scripture affirms this reality. Paul writes in Romans that "the whole creation has been groaning as in the pains of childbirth," and continues, "In the same way, the Spirit helps us in our weakness. We do not know what we ought to pray for, but the Spirit himself intercedes for us through wordless groans," (Romans 8:22-23). The created order groans with longing it cannot articulate. We, as image bearers living in that same groaning creation, often cannot articulate what we truly need or feel. God through the Holy Spirit translates the cries of our hearts into prayers. He prays for us when we lack words, with groanings too deep for human language.

My daughter illustrates this beautifully. She's nearly two, and while she's beginning to speak, her vocabulary is still limited. But her will and desires far exceed her ability to express them. She has strong opinions about everything, yet lacks the words to communicate them. Sometimes she tries desperately to tell us what she wants, gesturing wildly, using the few words she knows. When we still don't understand, she breaks down in tears of frustration.

In those moments, she has my heart completely. Her inability to articulate doesn't diminish my desire to help. If anything, it intensifies it. I lean in closer, trying harder to understand. Even when I can't figure out her exact request, I know what's good for her. I know what she needs.

This is how God listens when we pray. Our stumbling words, our wandering thoughts, our inability to articulate what we feel or need doesn't push God away. He's our Father, listening with the full attention of His infinite love.

"Through the praise of children and infants you have established a stronghold against your enemies, to silence the foe and the avenger." - Psalm 8:2

The Rational Trap

Satan knows how dangerous honest, faith-filled prayer is, so he works to redirect our thinking. He wants us to analyze prayer, dissect it, and ultimately dismiss it as unreasonable. This is the trap, getting us to intellectualize prayer until we stop actually praying.

One primary strategy is getting us to pray only for things that seem naturally achievable. Scripture commands us to pray for daily bread and for the healing of the sick. These are concrete, physical requests. But the rational mind reframes them into something safer. Instead of praying for actual provision, for money to pay bills or food on the table, we pray for "spiritual bread" or contentment. Instead of boldly asking God to heal cancer or restore damaged limbs, we hedge our requests with "comfort," or "God's will," or "strength to endure." These are legitimate prayers, but when they replace specific, bold requests, we're not praying in faith. We're praying in fear of looking foolish if God doesn't answer as we asked.

Yet even with evidence that prayer matters, the rational trap persists. I experienced this tension with a friend whose father received devastating medical news. The prognosis was grim. Everything in the natural order pointed to one inevitable outcome. The rational mind wants to craft prayers within the boundaries of what doctors say is possible. But faith doesn't operate that way. Doctors' prognoses don't define our hope. Yes, we face hard realities and make wise decisions based on medical information. But we don't let the limits of human knowledge define what we ask God to do.

Here's the reality, we don't know everything about the natural world. Medical science knows vastly more today than a century ago, but it still encounters cases that defy expectations. Our understanding remains limited. God, who created and sustains the natural order, operates with infinite knowledge and power. His ways are higher than our ways, His thoughts higher than our thoughts. The gap between what we understand and what God knows is infinite. To pray in faith isn't naive foolishness. It's a humble acknowledgment that God's resources infinitely exceed ours.

The rational trap also shows up after prayers are answered. We explain them away as a coincidence, as something that would have happened anyway. A few years ago, I prayed about a job opportunity that seemed perfect. After the second interview, I was confident I'd get an offer. I prayed for guidance. The third interview went sideways, with inappropriate questions from the CEO. I got the offer at my desired salary, but something felt wrong. I prayed again and felt led to decline. Weeks later, I met someone who'd worked there. When I mentioned turning down their offer, she said, "You made the best decision of your life. That place is a nightmare." My rational mind could dismiss this as luck or intuition. But looking back honestly, I saw God's hand protecting me, answering prayers.

I've seen this pattern often in my family. When I inventory the specific prayers we've brought to God over recent years, I'm struck by how many have been answered. The house we live in, the business opportunities that emerged, specific decisions that turned out far better than we could have planned. My rational mind wants to explain them away as good planning and hard work. But when I honestly assess it, I see the Lord's hand in every detail. The timing was too perfect. Doors opened in ways I couldn't have orchestrated. To dismiss these as a coincidence robs God of glory and weakens my faith for future prayers.

This is why prayer journals and shared testimonies matter. When we write down what we're praying for, we create a record our rational minds can't later explain away. When we pray together and celebrate together when God answers, we reinforce each other's faith. The demonic wants us isolated, quietly rationalizing away every answer until we stop believing prayer accomplishes anything. But when we pray in community and testify to God's work, we build each other up and resist the rational trap.

Faith calls us to approach God's throne with boldness, bringing requests to a Father whose wisdom and power infinitely exceed our understanding, and who delights to hear and answer His children's prayers.

A Sacred Privilege and Responsibility

A hymn captures prayer's heart better than any theological treatise, "What a friend we have in Jesus, all our sins and griefs to bear. What a privilege to carry everything to God in prayer." These simple words express something profound; prayer is both a great privilege and a sacred responsibility. It's a gift we've been given and something we're called to practice faithfully, whether we feel like it or not.

Think about life's greatest blessings, marriage, parenthood, meaningful work. Each is simultaneously joy and responsibility. Most days, being married is wonderful. But some days are hard, requiring sacrifice and choosing to love when you don't feel loving. In those moments, marriage becomes a responsibility you fulfill out of commitment. That's what makes it meaningful.

The same is true of parenting. Most days, spending time with my children is life's highlight. But at 2am when someone's sick, or during the fiftieth explanation of why we don't hit our sister, it doesn't feel like privilege. It feels like work, like a responsibility I must fulfill whether I want to or not. But that doesn't diminish its value. My commitment to parenting, even in hard moments, makes the relationship more meaningful.

Prayer works the same way. Some days, prayer flows naturally. You feel God's presence, words come easily, and you sense communion that fills you with joy and peace. But many days, prayer is harder. Your mind wanders. You're not sure what to say. You don't feel particularly close to God. In those moments, prayer becomes something you do out of obedience, not because it feels good. You pray because you're called to pray, because it matters. After all, it's part of your relationship with God, whether you feel like it or not. God honors both kinds of prayer. He delights in prayers flowing from overflowing hearts and hears prayers coming from simple obedience.

This means bringing everything to God in prayer. Not just spiritual things or what seems appropriate for religious conversation. Everything. Our daily bread, the money we need, job opportunities, and practical provisions. The healing of our sick, specific bold requests for God to intervene in failing bodies, grim diagnoses, situations that look hopeless by natural standards. Our relationships, fears, hopes, frustrations. Things that seem too small to bother God with and things that seem too big for Him to fix. All of it.

Scripture consistently encourages comprehensive prayer. We're told to cast all our anxieties on Him because He cares for us. All our anxieties. We're told to keep asking, keep seeking, keep knocking. The persistence itself matters. Repeatedly coming to God with the same request, refusing to give up, and determination to keep bringing our needs to our Father pleases Him.

> *"So I say to you, ask, and it will be given to you; seek, and you will find; knock, and it will be opened to you. For everyone who asks receives, and he who seeks finds, and to him who knocks it will be opened." - Luke 11:9-10.*

The Persistent Prayers of Groups

Researchers at Duke University Medical Center studied nearly four thousand elderly adults and found that those who attended religious services weekly were forty-six percent less likely to die over a six-year period than those who attended less frequently. The same research group found that regular prayer correlated with significantly lower blood pressure and healthier immune function.[1] These findings don't prove supernatural intervention, but they demonstrate that prayer has real, measurable effects. God works through natural means as well as supernatural ones. Prayer isn't abstract spirituality disconnected from the physical world.

Prayer is also uniquely Christian. Yet, in our culture, prayer gets lumped with meditation and mindfulness as if they're basically the same techniques for reducing stress or finding inner peace. But Christian prayer is fundamentally different. We're not just centering ourselves or achieving peaceful mental states. We're approaching a personal God who hears, cares, and responds. We're not manipulating spiritual forces. We're talking to our Father, who knows us, loves us, and has the power to act on our behalf.

Prayer is a muscle that strengthens with use. The more you pray, the more natural it becomes. The more you bring honest thoughts and feelings to God, the more comfortable you become with that vulnerability. The more you see Him answer prayers, the more your faith grows and the bolder your prayers become. Some days it flows easily. Some days it feels like work. But both kinds of days matter.

Takeaway

When your mind wanders during prayer, make that wandering the content of your prayer. Bring your distraction, your inability to

---

[1] Koenig, H.G., Hays, J.C., Larson, D.B., et al. "Does Religious Attendance Prolong Survival? A Six-Year Follow-up Study of 3,968 Older Adults." The Journals of Gerontology Series A: Biological Sciences and Medical Sciences, 1999. Koenig, H.G., Cohen, H.J., et al. "Attendance at Religious Services, Interleukin-6, and Other Biological Parameters of Immune Function in Older Adults." International Journal of Psychiatry in Medicine. Koenig, H.G. "Religion, Spirituality, and Health: The Research and Clinical Implications." ISRN Psychiatry, 2012.

focus, your scattered thoughts to God. He receives honest cries from struggling hearts far more readily than polished performances from prideful minds. When you lack words, trust that the Holy Spirit intercedes for you with groanings too deep for words. God doesn't require eloquence. He requires faith. Don't let rationalism rob you of bold prayer. God's wisdom and resources infinitely exceed yours. His ways are higher. What seems impossible to you may be trivial to Him. Pray for healing, provision, and unlikely outcomes. When God answers, don't dismiss it as a coincidence. Give Him glory.

Remember that prayer is both a privilege and a responsibility. What a privilege to carry everything to God in prayer. Bring your joys and sorrows, hopes and fears, victories, and failures. Bring things that seem too small to mention and things that seem too big to fix. Approach His throne with boldness, knowing you have a Father who hears, cares, and delights to answer His children's prayers.

A Closing Prayer

Dear Lord, thank you for the gift of prayer. Thank you, Jesus, for giving us access to the throne room of heaven to pour out our hearts. Holy Spirit, thank you for interceding for me when I don't have the words and I ask that you would strengthen me and fall on me to pray with your power. Thank you for listening to everything we bring to you. I ask that you would continue to teach me to pray. Take my prayer life deeper than ever before. Give me strength and discipline to seek you. And give me ears to hear when you are speaking. In Jesus name, Amen!

# Chapter 28
Salvation and Finishing Strong

In Letter 28, we encounter one of the most sobering moments in the entire correspondence. Screwtape rebukes Wormwood for celebrating the fact that the patient is in a war zone surrounded by bombs and danger. Screwtape essentially says, "What are you thinking?! If this man dies now, we've lost him. He's faithfully walking with Jesus even when times are difficult. If he dies today, he goes straight to heaven, and all our efforts have been wasted." The demonic strategy shifts dramatically at this point. Screwtape tells Wormwood to hope the patient survives the war and lives a long life, because Satan needs time. Seventy years, Screwtape notes, is not too long to slowly unknit a man's soul from heaven and build up a firm attachment to the world. This chapter addresses the long game of faith, the reality that Satan plays for keeps over the entire course of your life, and the critical distinction between God's work of preservation and our calling to persevere.

Scripture

"Blessed is the one who perseveres under trial because, having stood the test, that person will receive the crown of life that the Lord has promised to those who love him." - James 1:12

The Parable of the Sower: Satan's Long Game Strategy

When you read Letter 28 carefully, you can see that C. S. Lewis had a specific passage of Scripture in mind as he wrote. It's the Parable of the Sower, found in Matthew 13, Mark 4, and Luke 8. This parable maps out exactly what Screwtape describes as the demonic strategy for pulling established believers away from Christ over the course of a lifetime. Understanding this parable is essential to understanding this letter.

Jesus tells the story of a farmer scattering seed. Some seed falls along the path, and the birds immediately come and devour it. Jesus explains that this represents people who hear the word of the kingdom, but the evil one comes and snatches away what was sown in their hearts. This is the quick strike, the immediate attack. The demonic swoops in fast before the seed can even take root. For young believers or those just beginning to explore faith, Satan's primary tactic is speed. Snatch it up before it has a chance to grow.

But some seed falls on rocky ground where there isn't much soil. It springs up quickly, but the soil is shallow, and when the sun comes up, the plants are scorched and they wither. Jesus explains that this represents those who hear the word and receive it with joy, but they have no root in themselves. When trouble or persecution comes because of the word, they immediately fall away. This is adversity. This is when life gets hard, when following Jesus costs you something, when trials and tribulations test whether your faith has any depth.

Other seed falls among thorns. It starts to grow, but the thorns grow up and choke it, and it produces no grain. Jesus explains that this represents those who hear the word, but the cares of the world and the deceitfulness of riches and the desires for other things choke the word, and it proves unfruitful. This is prosperity. This is when life goes well, when you're successful, when you have comfort and abundance and all the things you thought would make you happy. Your faith gets crowded out by everything else competing for your attention.

Finally, some seed falls on good soil and produces a crop, some thirtyfold, some sixtyfold, some a hundredfold. This is the believer who perseveres all the way to the end, who produces fruit, who finishes the race strong.

Now look at what Screwtape is telling Wormwood. He's frustrated because the first tactic, the quick strike to snatch the seed before it takes root, has already failed. The patient has established faith. He's past that initial vulnerable stage. The seed has taken root. So Screwtape shifts strategy. He tells Wormwood to hope for a long life because now they have to employ the tactics of the second and third soils. They have to use either middle-aged adversity or middle-aged prosperity. These are the two primary weapons Satan uses against believers over the long haul of life.

Lewis describes the demonic as a calculated, strategic enemy. Satan has seventy years, maybe more, to slowly work on unknitting your soul from heaven. He doesn't need to destroy your faith in a single dramatic moment. He just needs time. Time to wear you down through trials. Time to distract you with success. Time to let the long, dull, monotonous years of middle age erode your passion and dull your spiritual senses. The demonic play the long game, and they're very, very patient.

The Demonic Perspective: A Tug of War?

Here's where things get theologically interesting, and we need to address it head-on. Throughout *The Screwtape Letters*, Lewis portrays the demonic realm as viewing salvation as something that's up for grabs. As if your eternal destiny is a tug of war that could go either way depending on who pulls harder. Screwtape genuinely seems to believe that, given enough time and the right tactics, they can pull the patient away from God and secure his soul for hell. This raises a crucial question: Did C. S. Lewis believe you could lose your salvation?

This is a conversation that has divided Christians for centuries, and we need to be careful and thoughtful here. The traditional Reformed or Calvinist position teaches eternal security, often summarized as "once saved, always saved." This theology emphasizes that salvation is entirely God's work. If God has truly saved you, if He has called you and regenerated your heart and justified you, then nothing can separate you from His love. Jesus said, "No one can snatch them out of my hand." That's not a suggestion. That's a promise. Salvation belongs to the Lord, and what God starts in you, He's determined to finish in you.

The Arminian position, on the other hand, emphasizes human free will and suggests that it's possible for someone to genuinely come to faith and then later fall away and lose their salvation. This view takes seriously the many warnings in Scripture about enduring to the end and not falling away from the faith.

So which view is correct? And more importantly for our purposes, which view did C. S. Lewis hold? The honest answer is that we don't know for certain what Lewis personally believed about eternal security. What we do know is that Lewis chose to portray the demonic as operating under the belief that salvation is contestable. Whether that reflects Lewis's actual theology or is simply a narrative choice to heighten the stakes and urgency of spiritual warfare, we can't say definitively.

But here's what I want you to understand. There's a way to hold both perspectives in tension that's actually incredibly helpful for how we live our Christian lives. You might be able to say, we should believe like Calvinists but act like Arminians. God knows who belongs to Him. God's purposes will not be thwarted. What God starts, He will finish. But the demonic realm operates as if the battle is still being fought, as if they still have a chance to pull you away from God if they just work hard enough and long enough.

And here's the thing, even if you're theologically convinced that you cannot lose your salvation, it's actually spiritually healthy to recognize that you're fighting an enemy who thinks he can win you. Satan is playing tug of war with your soul, whether or not that's theologically accurate. He's not sitting back saying, "Well, God has already determined who's elect, so I guess I'll just give up." No. He's fighting for every soul as if the outcome is in doubt.

This is where the practical rubber meets the theological road. In the courtroom of eternity, in the mind and purposes of God, your salvation may be absolutely secure if you truly belong to Christ. But in the trenches of daily spiritual warfare, you're fighting an enemy who has seventy years of tactics planned out to pull you away from Jesus. And the only way you know for certain that you're truly saved is if you finish the race. The only way to prove that seed fell on good soil is if it produces fruit all the way to harvest.

"Watch therefore, for you do not know what hour your Lord is coming. But know this, that if the master of the house had known what hour the thief would come, he would have watched and not allowed his house to be broken into. Therefore you also be ready, for the Son of Man is coming at an hour you do not expect." - Matthew 24:42-44

Perseverance vs. Preservation: Two Sides of One Coin

This brings us to the heart of the chapter and one of the most important distinctions in all of Christian theology, the difference between perseverance and preservation. These are two sides of the same coin, two aspects of the same reality, and understanding both is critical to living faithfully.

Preservation is God's work. This is what theologians call "the perseverance of the saints" or "the preservation of the saints." It's the doctrine that God preserves those who are truly His. He guards them. He keeps them. He works in them both to will and to work for His good pleasure. Philippians 1:6 says, "He who began a good work in you will carry it on to completion until the day of Christ Jesus." That's preservation. That's God's promise that what He starts, He finishes. No one can pluck you out of His hand. Your salvation does not ultimately depend on your ability to white knuckle your way through life and hold onto God. It depends on God holding onto you.

This is crucial to understand because your salvation is not 99.9% Jesus, and 0.01% you. If it were, you'd be doomed. You'd mess it up. Salvation is monergistic, meaning it's the work of one. It's God's work alone. The Bible is clear that we are dead in our trespasses and sins. We're not weak or sick. We're spiritually dead. And it is God alone who grants life. God regenerates hearts. God calls, justifies, sanctifies, and will one day glorify His people. That's preservation, and it's entirely His work.

But here's the other side of the coin, perseverance is our work. Not in the sense that we earn or maintain our salvation through our efforts, but in the sense that we are called to "work out our salvation with fear and trembling." We are commanded to make every effort to confirm our calling and election. We are told to examine ourselves to see if we are in the faith. We are instructed to take up our cross daily and follow Jesus. All the way through Scripture, we see both the security of God's preservation and the urgency of our perseverance held together in tension.

Paul can say, "It is no longer I who live, but Christ who lives in me," and in the very same breath say, "I press on toward the goal for the prize of the upward call of God in Christ Jesus." He can say, "Work out your own salvation with fear and trembling," and then immediately add, "for it is God who works in you, both to will and to work for his good pleasure." These aren't contradictions. They're complementary truths. God preserves us by working in us the very perseverance He calls us to exercise.

This is why the Christian life is described as running a race. You don't run a race by sitting on the sidelines congratulating yourself that God has predestined you to win. You run. You train. You discipline your body. You press on toward the goal. Yes, God has ordained the outcome, but He has also ordained the means. And the means involve you actually running the race. The life of faith is not a theological exam where you get the right answers and then coast. It's a daily battle. It's a marathon that requires endurance, discipline, and perseverance all the way to the finish line.

Here's the test that the apostle John gives us, "They went out from us, but they were not of us; for if they had been of us, they would have continued with us. But they went out, that it might become plain that they all are not of us." The people who fall away and don't come back, who abandon the faith and never return, were never truly part of the family to begin with. But the only way you know if you're truly part of God's family is by staying. By persevering. By finishing the race. Life is not a sprint. It's a marathon. The question is not just whether you started the race well. The question is whether you'll finish strong.

Middle Aged Adversity and Prosperity

Lewis describes middle age with a phrase that should stop us in our tracks, "the long, dull, monotonous years." If you're in middle-aged or approaching it, you know exactly what he means. The excitement and passion of youth have faded. The energy you once had for spiritual things feels harder to maintain. Life settles into routines. You wake up, go to work, pay the bills, deal with the stress, try to keep your family together, and fall into bed exhausted. Repeat. Day after day. Year after year. The long, dull, monotonous years.

This is exactly the battlefield Screwtape is describing. This is where Satan does his most effective work, not in the dramatic moments but in the slow erosion of the everyday. He has two primary weapons for this stage of life, and they correspond exactly to the second and third soils in Jesus's parable: adversity and prosperity.

Middle-aged adversity is the rocky soil. These are the trials and difficulties and hardships that just wear you down over time. Maybe it's a difficult marriage that never quite gets better. Maybe it's financial stress that never seems to end. Maybe it's health problems, aging parents, wayward children, job loss, chronic pain, disappointment after disappointment. When you're young, trials can actually strengthen your faith. They drive you to God. But when you're middle-aged and you've been dealing with the same struggles for twenty years with no end in sight, adversity can crush you. It can make you bitter. It can make you question whether God really cares. It can wear away your faith like water eroding stone, slowly, imperceptibly, until one day you realize you're faith is gone.

Middle-aged prosperity is the thorny soil. These are the cares and pleasures and successes that crowd out your spiritual life. You work hard, you build a career, you achieve financial stability, you buy a nice house in a good neighborhood, your kids are doing well in school, you have time for hobbies and travel and all the things you always wanted to do. Life is good. Really good. And subtly, almost imperceptibly, your need for God diminishes. You still go to church occasionally. You still might pray before meals. You still identify as a Christian. But Jesus becomes a distant memory, someone you met years ago, and you wanted Him more. Your heart gets knit to the earth. You invest all your time and energy and passion into building a comfortable life here, and heaven becomes an abstract concept you'll deal with someday.

Both of these are deadly. Both of them slowly unknit your soul from heaven. And both of them require time to work their effects. This is why perseverance matters so much. You can't live today on the spiritual victories of yesterday. You can't coast on the faith you had five years ago or ten years ago or twenty years ago. Every day requires fresh dependence on God. Every season of life brings new challenges and new temptations. You have to keep running the race. You have to keep fighting the fight. You have to keep taking up your cross daily.

There's a prayer in Proverbs that captures this perfectly. "Give me neither poverty nor riches but give me only my daily bread. Otherwise, I may have too much and disown you and say, 'Who is the Lord?' Or I may become poor and steal, and so dishonor the name of my God." [2]Don't let me be so crushed by adversity that I compromise and dishonor your name. And don't let me be so prosperous that I forget I need you. Keep me dependent. Keep me humble. Keep me close.

That's the prayer of someone who understands the long game. That's the prayer of someone who knows that Satan will use either

---

adversity or prosperity to try to pull them away from God. That's the prayer of someone committed to persevering all the way to the end.

Takeaway

The Christian life is not a sprint. It's a marathon. Satan doesn't give up after your first year of faith. He has a seventy-year strategy for your life, and he's incredibly patient. He'll use adversity to crush you or prosperity to distract you. He'll exploit the long, dull, monotonous years to slowly erode your passion for God. He plays the long game, and he plays for keeps.

But here's the good news, God preserves those who are His. What He starts, He finishes. Your salvation ultimately rests not on your ability to hold onto God but on God's power to hold onto you. That's the security you can rest in. That's the hope that sustains you through every trial and every season.

And yet, you are called to persevere. You are called to work out your salvation with fear and trembling. You are called to examine yourself, to fight the fight of faith, to press on toward the goal, to run the race with endurance. You can't coast. You can't presume. You can't bank on yesterday's faith to carry you through today's battles. The same faith that brought you to salvation on day one is the faith you need to exercise every single day until you cross the finish line.

A Closing Prayer

Heavenly Father, I am forever grateful for the gift of salvation through Your Son, Jesus Christ, a grace I could never deserve. Grant me the strength to run my race with perseverance, that I may honor You and live worthy of the calling of a child of God. Draw me closer to You. Be with me through the temptations of worldly pleasures and the difficult trials of life. Fix my eyes on You, Lord, and keep my heart Yours forever. Empower me through Your Holy Spirit to share the joy I find in Jesus with others. Let the Spirit guide and protect me as I live for You. In Jesus' name, Amen.

Chapter 29
Courage in the Face of Fear

When circumstances become dire and evil undeniable, something shifts in the human heart. The trivial concerns that occupied our minds during comfortable times suddenly fade away. What truly matters comes into sharp focus. Crisis has a way of stripping away everything superficial and forcing us to confront reality.

In Letter 29, Screwtape faces this problem as the patient lives through war and destruction. The demonic tactics that work during peacetime become useless when good and evil stand in stark contrast. Trials don't make a man; they reveal him. And right now, the church is being revealed. We're facing our own test of character. The question is simple, Will we respond with courage or cowardice? With love or hatred?

Scripture

"Have I not commanded you? Be strong and courageous. Do not be afraid; do not be discouraged, for the Lord your God will be with you wherever you go." - Joshua 1:9

You Are in a Battle, Like it or Not

Most people reading this book aren't living in an active war zone. You're not dodging bombs or running from soldiers. But that doesn't mean you're not in a battle. The war you're fighting is spiritual, ideological, and cultural. It's a battle for truth in a world that calls good evil and evil good. It's a battle to raise children in righteousness when every cultural force pulls them toward destruction. It's a battle to stand firm when speaking biblical truth can cost you everything. Paul writes that we do not wrestle against flesh and blood, but against rulers, authorities, and spiritual forces of evil. This isn't metaphorical. You are engaged in spiritual warfare right now. The question isn't whether you're in the battle. The question is whether you're willing to fight or will sit on the sidelines pretending the battle doesn't exist.

War, revolution, and threshold moments force us to see clearly. When life is comfortable, we can debate endlessly about gray areas. We can convince ourselves that there are no absolute truths. But when you're facing genuine evil that wants to destroy everything good, philosophical handwringing becomes impossible. It's a test, a crucible to forge our moral fortitude. You know what's true. You know what matters. You know which side you're on.

Here's a test. Do you feel called to courage? If you don't, then you're not ready to fight. Courage is only required when there's something at stake, when standing firm means standing against opposition. If your Christian life feels comfortable and safe, it's because you're not confronting the evil that surrounds you. You're retreating far enough that the battle hasn't reached you yet, but it will.

Wherever your actual battle is, that's where your courage will be tested. Maybe it's in the realm of ideas, standing for truth, where lies are celebrated. Maybe it's in business, refusing to compromise integrity even at financial cost. Maybe it's in your family, having difficult conversations about righteousness. Maybe it's in your church, calling out compromise and demanding biblical faithfulness. Whatever arena God has placed you in, that's your battlefield.

Courage Is Required

Let's recall what courage actually is. Courage is not the absence of fear. It's not a feeling of confidence. Courage is acting rightly despite fear. It's doing what you're called to do, even when you're terrified. It's standing firm when everything in your flesh wants to run. This distinction matters enormously. If we think courage means not feeling afraid, we'll wait to act until we feel brave. And that day will never come.

C. S. Lewis understood this profoundly. He points out through Screwtape that courage is not simply one of the virtues, "but the form of every virtue at the testing point." Think about what this means. You might claim to love truth, but if you're not willing to speak truth when it costs you something, then you don't actually love truth. You love comfort. Every virtue we claim to possess will be tested at some point, and courage is what allows those virtues to be real when the test comes.

The temptation when fear grips us is to negotiate with it. We spin out scenarios, trying to find some path that avoids the cost. If this happens, I'll do that. If they threaten this, I'll compromise on that. We're trying to maintain control, to navigate danger without actually having to stand firm. But this is the path of the coward. Real courage requires us to stop negotiating and simply focus on duty. What am I called to do? What does obedience require? Then we do that thing, regardless of consequences, trusting God with the outcome.

Fear is contagious. We saw this during COVID. A virus spread through the population, but fear spread even faster. Fear of death, of disease, of economic collapse, of being canceled for asking questions, and it led to profound damage. People surrendered freedoms, turned on neighbors, and compromised convictions. All because fear spread like a plague.

But courage is also contagious. When you see someone stand firm in the face of opposition, it inspires something deep in your soul. When you watch someone refuse to back down even when threatened, it awakens courage in you. There's an inherent beauty in courage that resonates with our humanity, that reminds us of who we were created to be. This is what it means to be strong and courageous as God commands. The fear will come. The discouragement will come. But you act courageously anyway because God is with you. Not that you'll feel brave, but that God will be with you in the battle.

Hatred is Cowardly

When you're under intense pressure and fear grips you, your emotional regulation becomes compromised. This is exactly when the enemy wants to push you toward hatred.

Lewis describes this brilliantly. "Hatred is the compensation by which a frightened man reimburses himself for the miseries of fear." When fear makes you feel weak, hatred gives you a sense of power back. You can't control the threats coming, but you can hate with intensity that feels like fighting back. But it's a trap, the enemy's way of destroying you even while you think you're fighting him.

We can and should hate evil. Romans 12:9 says, "Abhor what is evil; hold fast to what is good." There is righteous hatred of wickedness. But there's a crucial distinction between hating evil and hating enemies. Jesus commands us to love our enemies and pray for

268

those who persecute us. This isn't optional. The challenge is maintaining that distinction under fire. When someone threatens what you love, the natural response is to hate them. But we're not animals driven by instinct. We're made in God's image, called to something higher, capable of loving enemies even while we oppose their evil.

James writes that the wrath of man does not accomplish the righteousness of God. If we let anger turn into hatred and uncontrolled rage, we're not advancing God's kingdom. Hatred doesn't defeat evil, it spreads evil. It makes us like what we're fighting. Both cowardice and hatred lead to shame. In the heat of battle, hatred feels powerful. But once you're emotionally regulated, you see what fear made you become, that you responded with the same viciousness as your enemy.

This is the distinction we must maintain. We hate evil and oppose it with everything we have. But we love the sinner, seeing them as image bearers who need redemption. Even while we fight against what they're doing, we pray for their salvation.

Standing Firm

Scripture tells us to act justly, love mercy, and walk humbly with God. These aren't abstract ideals. They're concrete actions we're called to embody. But here's what we often miss, you can only actually do these things if you're willing to stand courageously for them. It's easy to talk about justice when justice is popular. The test comes when doing these things requires courage, when standing for justice means standing against the crowd.

We are biblically called to confront evil. This isn't optional. Every follower of Christ is called to stand against wickedness and stand for righteousness. We're told to expose the works of darkness. We're told not to participate in evil but to oppose it. If we claim to follow Jesus but won't stand for what He stands for when standing costs us something, then our faith is mere words with no substance.

The church is being tested right now. We're encountering evils that demand a response. A culture that celebrates the murder of children. A movement that confuses children about basic reality and pushes them toward permanent mutilation. An educational system that teaches children to hate truth. A media complex that lies constantly and punishes those who expose the lies. These aren't abstract problems. They're attacks on everything good and true. And the question before us is: Will we stand?

Charlie Kirk stood tall with courage, firm in Christ, despite relentless threats. He refused to yield to fear or hatred, keeping his focus on God's truth. He never wavered. The enemy could not tolerate his influence. Their mistake, his faith led him home to the Lord in glory, free from the grip of the demonic, welcomed by God's grace. People who were silent are speaking. People who were comfortably content are now engaging. The blood of martyrs truly is the seed of the church. His death now places a solemn call on each of us, what will you do? Will you stand in prayer and say, "God, here I am!"?[3]

Courage matters all the way to the end. 2 Timothy 4:7, "I have fought the good fight, I have finished the race, I have kept the faith." We don't know which day will be our testing point or our last. So, we must be ready always, resolved always, determined always to stand firm in faith and courage, no matter the cost.

This is what Jesus meant when He said we must take up our cross daily and follow Him. The cross isn't metaphorical for minor inconvenience. It's the symbol of total sacrifice, of loving righteousness more than life itself. Jesus endured the cross for us. He

---

[3] Isaiah 6:8

faced the ultimate test with perfect courage, perfect love, perfect faithfulness. And He calls us to follow Him on that path.

Takeaway

Be strong and courageous. Do not be afraid. Do not be discouraged. For the Lord, your God is with you wherever you go. This command echoes through Scripture and history. It's the call on your life right now. Be strong. Be courageous. Stand firm. Keep the faith. Love your enemies even while abhorring their evil. Stay emotionally regulated. Don't let fear drive you to cowardice or hatred. Trust God with the outcome. And stand.

Closing Prayer

My God in heaven, make me strong in faith, discerning truth in this world, and willing to lose anything to gain everything in You. When I am weak, forgive me, strengthen me, and give me courage to put on the full armor of God. Let me fight my battle well, picking up the sword of truth with courage to take into the fight against evil. Let me keep your commandments fearlessly. Help me to bravely speak the name of Jesus, resist the enemy, and stand firm for You! In Christ's name, Amen.

Chapter 30
Strong in the Lord

Life has a way of pushing us beyond what we think we can handle. Whether it's the relentless demands of parenting, financial pressures that won't let up, prolonged illness, workplace stress, or the emotional weight of caring for aging parents, we all face seasons where we're running on empty. We hit our limit. Our reserves are depleted. The tank is dry. These are the moments when our faith is truly tested, when our character is revealed, and when the enemy sees his greatest opportunity. Fatigue doesn't just make us tired. It makes us vulnerable. Our judgment becomes impaired, our patience runs thin, and sins we'd normally resist suddenly seem more appealing. The question isn't whether we'll face these seasons of exhaustion, but how we'll respond when we do. Will we rely on our own diminishing strength, or will we discover what it means to be strong in the Lord when we have nothing left to give?

Scripture

"But he said to me, "My grace is sufficient for you, for my power is made perfect in weakness." Therefore I will boast all the more gladly about my weaknesses, so that Christ's power may rest on me. That is why, for Christ's sake, I delight in weaknesses, in insults, in hardships, in persecutions, in

difficulties. For when I am weak, then I am strong." - 2 Corinthians 12:9-10

The Reality of Fatigue

In Lewis's thirtieth letter, the patient finds himself surrounded by carnage and devastation. He's witnessed horrors, human remains blasted against walls, friends killed beside him, the constant threat of death. He's terrified and exhausted, pushed far beyond what any person should endure. Yet remarkably, he hasn't despaired. He's still doing his duty, acting rightly despite his fear. His circumstances have driven him to humility, stripping away the raw material the demonic forces need to tempt him effectively.

Most of us won't find ourselves in literal battlefields, but we will face circumstances that push us to our limits. The young mother who hasn't slept through the night in months. The man facing mounting bills and dwindling savings. The woman caring for aging parents while raising her own children. The employee enduring a toxic work environment. The person walking through prolonged illness or chronic pain. These aren't minor inconveniences, they drain us physically, emotionally, mentally, and spiritually.

Growth happens at the edge of our capacity, not in the comfort zone. Just as muscles only grow when broken down through resistance training, our spiritual strength develops when we're pushed to our limit. We shouldn't be at our limit all the time, but we should get there from time to time.

But fatigue is dangerous. When we're depleted, we become far more susceptible to temptation and sin. Our judgment becomes impaired. Things that would normally horrify us start to seem reasonable. That sharp word flies out. That ethical compromise suddenly looks practical. Fatigue creates vulnerabilities the enemy is eager to exploit.

This is why Paul's instruction to "be strong in the Lord and in the power of His might"[4] appears in Ephesians right before he discusses spiritual warfare. When you're tired, depleted, at your limit, you cannot rely on your own strength. The true test of valor comes at our weakest moments, when we're weary and worn down, and we still choose to do what's right because we're relying on God's power rather than our own.

The Demonic Trap of "Reasonable" Endurance

We all know we should endure hardship and persevere. But how much is enough? How long should we endure before we're justified in giving up? This is one of the most devastating demonic traps. Satan doesn't need to convince you that commitment is bad, he just needs to convince you that unlimited commitment is unreasonable.

Once you start measuring your endurance against what seems reasonable, the demonic forces have won. They've shifted the standard from eternal to temporal, from total commitment to conditional faithfulness.

The trap is subtle. "Yes, you should persevere and be faithful. But only up to a point. Only for a reasonable amount of time. Only while certain conditions are met." When we hold permanent commitments to temporary standards, we set ourselves up for failure.

---

[4] Ephesians 6:10

Consider the model of Jesus. Scripture tells us that for the joy set before him, he endured the cross, even death on a cross. The most brutal, humiliating, agonizing form of execution ever devised. No conditions. No time limits. No threshold of pain that would justify turning back. Total commitment from before the foundation of the world to the very end. This is the standard we're called to mirror.

We see this trap devastate marriages today. When a couple vows "till death do us part," they're making a permanent commitment. But Satan whispers, "Yes, you should work on your marriage. But only up to a point. If things get bad enough, if it lasts long enough, then you're justified in walking away." That appeal to reasonableness is what causes countless marriages to collapse. The same principle applies to our children, our calling, or faith itself.

Sometimes, when people are pushed to their absolute limit, they fall into despair-driven sins. Young women facing desperate situations turn to prostitution or OnlyFans. Young men turn to gambling, pornography, or substance abuse. These are what happens when fatigue, hopelessness, and the enemy's lies converge, when people measure their lives by immediate circumstances instead of eternal standards.

The call is to maintain an eternal perspective. We don't endure hardship because it will definitely end soon. We endure because we're called to endure. We keep our commitments because those commitments reflect the unchanging character of God. We stay faithful because faithfulness isn't measured by duration or difficulty, it's measured by obedience to the One who calls us. "Be strong in the Lord and in the power of His might." Not your might. Not your assessment of what's reasonable. His might.

Hope, Perseverance, and "One More Day"

Proverbs gives us a penetrating insight, "Hope deferred makes the heart sick, but desire fulfilled is a tree of life."[5] When relief seems to be coming but never quite arrives, our hearts grow sick and weak. This is exactly the state the enemy wants to cultivate because hopelessness destroys our capacity to persevere.

In the 1950s, researcher Curt Richter placed wild rats into jars of water from which they couldn't escape. Despite their strength, these fierce animals gave up and drowned within just a few minutes. They assessed the situation, determined there was no hope, and surrendered to death. But then Richter modified the experiment. He placed other rats in the same situation, and just before they were about to drown, he pulled them out, dried them off, let them rest, and placed them back in the water. The results were astonishing. These rats swam for sixty hours or more.[6] What changed? They had experienced rescue. They now believed that even though they couldn't save themselves, salvation might come. As Richter wrote, "After elimination of hopelessness, the rats do not die." Hope didn't just extend their endurance slightly, it multiplied it from minutes to days.

Spiritual warfare is largely a battle of the mind. What we believe about our situation profoundly impacts our ability to endure it. Satan doesn't necessarily need to make our circumstances worse; he just needs to convince us they're hopeless.

---

[5] Proverbs 13:12

[6] *Learn something interesting: the Harvard University Hope Experiment.* (2021, June 2). Learn Something Interesting.
https://learnsomethinginteresting.com/2021/03/23/the-harvard-university- hope-experiment/

Consider the prophet Daniel, who fasted and prayed for three weeks seeking understanding. For twenty-one days, he heard nothing from heaven. What he didn't know was that an angel had been dispatched from the very first day, but demonic forces were blocking the angel's path. Daniel could have given up on day fourteen or quit on day twenty. But he persevered, and on day twenty-one, the breakthrough came. The angel arrived and said, "From the first day that you set your heart to understand and humbled yourself before your God, your words were heard, and I have come because of your words." The answer was on its way the entire time.

When you hit your limit, when you think you absolutely cannot go on, give it one more day. Hold out for one more week. You don't know what God can do in twenty-four hours. You don't know how close breakthrough might be.

Sometimes hope is fulfilled when God grants breakthrough. Other times, hope is fulfilled through His grace to endure. We cannot make hope itself an idol. Our ultimate hope cannot rest in our circumstances changing. Some people endure suffering their entire lives. Some relief never comes in this lifetime. The hope that sustains us must be hope in the Lord Himself, the confidence that whether our circumstances change or not, God is sovereign, God is good, and God will accomplish His purposes. When our hope is in Him rather than in our circumstances, we find that His grace is sufficient even when relief never comes.

Physical Facts and Spiritual Truth

Lewis makes a profound observation about how demonic forces manipulate our perspective. They don't need to lie to us outright; they simply need to get us to see only half of reality at a time.

There are empirical facts and spiritual truths. The enemy's tactic is to get us to dismiss one in order to overemphasize the other.

When we're going through intense hardship, Satan wants us to look at our circumstances and say, "This pain is what's really true. All that talk about God's goodness was naive fantasy." He wants us to dismiss spiritual truth and see only the physical facts. A soldier returns from war having seen the worst of humanity and becomes cynical. He's not wrong that war is horrific. He's wrong in thinking that horror is the only truth that matters.

But Satan plays the opposite game just as effectively. When we're comfortable, he wants us to dismiss the physical realities of suffering. "This comfort is what really matters. Don't burden yourself with suffering or sacrifice. That's all just religious negativity." He gets us to see only half the picture again, just a different half.

Consider how Satan tempted Jesus in the wilderness. He presented empirical facts, "You're hungry. These are stones. You have the power to turn them into bread." He was telling the truth about the circumstances, but Jesus responded with spiritual truth, "Man shall not live by bread alone, but by every word that comes from the mouth of God." Both are true. Hunger is real. But spiritual reality is equally real and ultimately more important.

The mature Christian learns to see both realities simultaneously without dismissing either one. Yes, war is horrific. Yes, suffering is real. Those are physical facts, and we don't minimize them. But it's equally true that beauty exists, that redemption is real, that God is at work bringing restoration. The soldier who returns from war can choose to become bitter, seeing only darkness and dismissing all beauty as naive. Or he can become better, seeing both the darkness and the beauty with deeper appreciation. You can get bitter or you can get better. The choice comes down to whether you'll let Satan isolate one reality from the other or whether you'll insist on seeing the whole picture.

When fatigue sets in, our perspective becomes especially vulnerable to this manipulation. Exhaustion makes us prone to darkness. We start seeing only the problems, only the pain. We forget that God is equally real in the midst of our suffering. The call is to see clearly, with sober, balanced, wise eyes that acknowledge the full truth of our situation. Yes, you're exhausted. Yes, the struggle is real. And yes, God's grace is sufficient. Yes, His power is made perfect in weakness. Yes, when you are weak, then in Him you are strong.

Takeaway

Fatigue will come if you're living fully and engaging meaningfully with the challenges of life. When you hit your limit, three crucial responses will determine whether you emerge stronger or broken.

First, commit totally rather than reasonably. Permanent commitments deserve permanent faithfulness. Total commitment means you'll stay faithful whether the hardship lasts a month or a lifetime. Second, hold out hope, but anchor that hope in the right place. You don't know what one more day can bring. When you hit your limit, give it one more day. But remember, your ultimate hope cannot be in your circumstances changing. It must be in the Lord Himself. Third, see clearly. Don't let fatigue twist your perspective so you see only darkness. Both your suffering and God's sovereignty are real. Both matter.

The secret to enduring when you hit your limit is found in Paul's instruction, "Be strong in the Lord and in the power of His might." (Ephesians 6:10) Not your strength. His might. His power. His strength working through your weakness. His grace is sufficient for you. His power is made perfect in your weakness. When you are weak, then in Him you are strong.

A Closing Prayer

Our Father in heaven, help me persevere through life, facing the trials and tribulations of my story with resilience and steadfast faith. When I am weak, give me strength to endure suffering. When I feel abandoned, remind me that you are near, already at work within me, never far from my distress. When I cry out and hear no answer, help me trust that you have heard my prayer. Let me run my race with endurance, all the way to the finish, without wavering or doubting your goodness and love. Amen.

Chapter 31
When Heaven Rejoices

In the final chapter of our journey through spiritual warfare, we arrive at the moment where life and faith culminate: death itself. Not as an ending, but as a doorway. Not as defeat, but as liberation. This is the moment when everything the enemy meant for evil, God redeems for good.

In Letter 31, the patient dies in a German air raid. One moment he is alive, the next he's entering into eternity. In that instant, he glimpsed Wormwood and the demons he most assuredly doubted existed. The evil ones who worked so hard to claim his soul watch as he slips through their fingers. Screwtape writes of the howl echoing through hell as another soul escapes their grasp. No longer can they attempt to separate him from God. As the demons faded beneath a celestial chorus, the patient fell into the arms of angels at the gates of Heaven. This is where his earthly struggles dissolved into a radiant meeting with the Lord. It was glorious.

Death entered into the world through sin, it was never God's design, and He is working to destroy it forever. Through Jesus Christ, death becomes the very thing that delivers us to God. This paradox defines Christian hope and gives life meaning. We grieve with tears but not without purpose. Death stings, but it doesn't have the final word. For the believer, heaven rejoices, hell despairs, we are home!

Scripture

"It was now about the sixth hour, and there was darkness over the whole land until the ninth hour, while the sun's light failed. And the curtain of the temple was torn in two. Then Jesus, calling out with a loud voice, said, "Father, into your hands I commit my spirit!" And having said this He breathed his last." - Luke 23:44-46

Death's Sting is Real

Before we talk about victory, we must acknowledge the pain. Death hurts, regardless of how or at what age our loved ones died. It stings even for those who believe with absolute certainty that they know where their loved ones have gone.

When Jesus learned His friend Lazarus had died, He wept. Not because He doubted the resurrection or lacked faith, but because death is an enemy, because separation cuts deep, because the people He loved were grieving. Even though He was moments away from raising Lazarus from the tomb, Jesus still wept. The tears were real, the grief legitimate.

The demonic want us to grieve with despair, to let sorrow crush us completely. And while we do grieve, we do not grieve as those who have no hope (1 Thessalonians 4:13). We embrace the pain while holding fast to hope, leaning on the Holy Spirit who comforts us and on Jesus who guarantees our victory even as we feel the sting.

Death separates us from loved ones here on earth, and that separation is genuinely painful. We don't minimize it or spiritualize it away with platitudes like "they're in a better place, so you shouldn't be sad." That's neither compassionate, pastoral, nor biblical. Jesus Himself demonstrated a different response to death.

The sting is real, but it's not final. The pain is legitimate, but it's not permanent. We feel the full weight of loss without being crushed by it, because we know something the demonic can never comprehend: death has been defeated.

The Battle for the Last Breath

The enemy doesn't surrender. Even in our final moments, the battle for our souls continues. This theological reality cannot be ignored, the demonic realm fights for each of us until our last breath. Perseverance of the saints isn't about a moment of initial zeal, but about enduring faith that carries us all the way home.

Every tactic we've examined in this book culminates in this final assault at death's door. But when we hold fast to Christ, when we persevere in faith, the demonic despair contrasts sharply with our joyous ascension. This is the moment when everything clicks into divine clarity. The confusion lifts. The warfare ends. We see what we've been fighting for all along.

We know this because we've witnessed it firsthand.

Ian: My mother lived a difficult life, but she spent her final years serving faithfully in the church. When an embolism caused her to fall down the stairs, her body was shattered. She lay in a pool of blood for hours before being discovered and rushed to the hospital. Two of my brothers sat vigil as doctors explained there was little hope. In her semi-conscious state, my mother whispered, "I don't want to die, but if it's my time, then so be it."

It was her time. The Father called her home.

The night before the funeral, my three brothers and I were sitting in my mother's living room, reminiscing. My younger brother, who considered himself an atheist and had been at her bedside, exclaimed through his tears, "I saw angels take her away." We were stunned. But what a message the Lord sent us, even through someone without faith. A wayward brother's angelic vision became a testimony to those who doubt. In that moment, the veil between physical and spiritual realities lifted just enough for an unbeliever to see truth. The demonic forces that had worked on my mother throughout her life, trying to keep her from God, lost. And in their defeat, they couldn't even hide it from someone who didn't believe they existed.

Galen: We also faced death as a family when my wife's mother battled cancer. She had fought it for several years, defeating it to the point of complete remission. But it returned, and this time it came back stronger than before, more aggressive, more unrelenting.

In the final months and weeks of her life, we learned things about grief and death that you can only learn by walking through the valley. We learned that love doesn't make death easier; it makes it harder. We learned that faith doesn't remove the pain; it gives you something to hold onto while you feel it. We learned that saying goodbye is one of the most sacred things humans do, and one of the most difficult.

We were profoundly grateful that my wife could spend those final weeks with her mother. Not everyone gets that gift. Not everyone has the chance to be present, to speak the words that need to be said, to hold the hand that held theirs when they were small. My wife was able to usher her mother all the way to the gates of heaven. That's the only way to describe it. She walked with her through the pain, through the fear, through the moments of clarity and the moments of confusion. She prayed over her. She sang over her. She read Scripture to her. She reminded her of God's promises. She held her hand. And when the final breath came, my wife was there, alongside her father, as her mother passed peacefully into the arms of Jesus.

There's something profoundly beautiful about being present for that moment, even as it breaks your heart. The pain is real. The tears are real. The sorrow cuts deep. But woven through all of it is something else entirely: hope. Peace. Even, somehow, joy. Not joy that she was leaving, but joy that she was arriving. Not happiness about the goodbye, but gratitude for the hello waiting on the other side. My wife describes it now as a uniquely precious time in her life, not because death is pleasant, but because being present for that sacred transition, that final moment of faith made visible, changed something in her. She saw her mother fight all the way to the end. She saw her mother cling to Jesus. She saw what it looks like when someone finishes the race well.

Both of these stories reveal the same truth, the battle rages until the very last moment, but for those who belong to Christ, victory is assured. This is the beauty of fighting all the way to the last breath.

Finding Meaning in the Fight

My son plays baseball, and even if you're the biggest baseball fan imaginable, consider what a game with no end would be like. Just endless innings that never result in a conclusion. There would be ups and downs, highlights and lowlights, but eventually you'd agree it was pointless. Without finality, nothing has weight. Without death, life has no measure.

Death gives life meaning. It creates urgency. It forces us to ask what truly matters. It reminds us that our days are numbered and our choices have consequences.

This has profound implications for how we live. The longer we live faithfully, the more we can accomplish for the kingdom, advancing the gospel, serving others, growing in holiness. The Bible speaks of rewards in heaven, of hearing "Well done, good and faithful servant," (Matthew 25:21)

The enemy's goal has never wavered. From the Garden of Eden to the present day, the demonic strategy is singular: separate you from God by any means necessary. But the tactics evolve. The methods adapt. The weapons get updated for each generation.

This is why we wrote *Confronting Evil in Our Time*. Not as an academic exercise, but as a tool of awareness to help you combat the enemy and live a blessed life. The tactics we've examined aren't historical curiosities. They're active right now, adapting to our modern world, exploiting our new vulnerabilities.

Don't just survive. Fight. Don't just avoid sin. Pursue holiness. Don't just believe the gospel. Live it out with courage and conviction. Confront the evil of our day with wisdom, with grace, with unshakable faith in the One who already won the war.

One day, God will wipe every tear from our eyes. There will be no more death or mourning or crying or pain, for the old order of things will pass away. Revelation 21 promises us this future. But that day is not today. Today, we live in the tension. Today, we fight the good fight. Today, we stand firm.

The power of the cross doesn't change. The victory of the resurrection doesn't fade. The promise that those who endure to the end will be saved remains as true today as it was two thousand years ago. No matter how sophisticated the demonic tactics become, they cannot overcome the simple truth of faith in Jesus Christ.

So, stand firm. Finish the race. Keep the faith. And when that final moment comes, let it find you faithful.

Closing

We would be remiss if we came all this way and didn't ask the question: Do you know the One who defeated death? Not just know *about* Him, but know Him personally?

Throughout these letters, we've examined spiritual warfare from many angles. But it all comes back to this:

Do you know Jesus?

Here's the gospel in its simplest form: Jesus Christ, the sinless Son of God, lived a perfect life we could never live. He died on the cross, taking the punishment for our sins. Three days later, He rose again, defeating death. This is the historical, life-changing truth of the gospel.

Salvation isn't about being good enough. It's about faith in Jesus Christ. Period.

If you've never put your faith in Jesus, you can do that right now. Pray something like this:

"Lord Jesus, I am a sinner. You are a sinless Savior. I put my faith in You. I believe You are the Son of God who died on the cross for my sins and rose again to defeat death. I trust You for salvation."

These aren't magic words. It's the posture of your heart toward Christ that matters.

If you prayed that prayer and truly meant it, welcome home. You've been delivered from death to life. And the ones who belong to Christ will live forever.

Thank you and may God bless you.

Afterword

How This Book Came to Be

Growing up in Coventry, England, I would frequently visit the iconic Coventry Cathedral, a site of profound historical and spiritual significance. On the exterior of the new cathedral is a sculpture a depiction of St. Michael triumphing over the devil. It is a powerful image. As a youth, this sculpture served as a stark reminder of the eternal struggle between good and evil and the belief in angelic forces beyond the earthly realm.

I have many questions for God and long to meet him face-to-face to ask him directly. For those of us who have experienced raising children, "Why?" is the beginning of most of their early questions, just like mine to God. The more I read and understand Scripture, the deeper it becomes, opening doors to deeper meaning and clarity around the "Why."

The prayer Jesus taught His disciples, and us, to pray was clear about the role evil would play in our lives saying, "Deliver us from…" In this passage, Jesus affirms the reality of evil and the inevitability of humanity's encounter with it in its most unfiltered form, emphasizing that the devil and demonic forces are not only real but actively present in the world. Even Jesus was led into demonic temptation during His incarnate life on earth, and at His crucifixion. He spoke with authority as the Son of God and used scripture as a shield to counter the devil's temptations.

It's worth noting that a phrase in the Lord's prayer regarding evil has been subject to different translations and interpretations by biblical scholars throughout the ages. Many translations today render the words of Jesus as "deliver us from evil," while other translations offer more interpretation of his phrase by stating "deliver us from the evil one." The original Greek could be interpreted either way, and scholars have debated which translation is more accurate. Whatever the case, it is clear that Jesus battled more than just a general sense of evil; He was directly tempted by Satan himself.

Many Christians sadly neglect regular engagement with Scripture, overlooking its vital role in spiritual formation. If they immersed themselves more deeply in the Word, they would come to understand that Scripture speaks powerfully to the reality of spiritual warfare. Ephesians 6:12 states, "For we wrestle not against flesh and blood, but against principalities, against powers, against the rulers of the darkness of this world, against spiritual wickedness in high places." This verse emphasizes that the Christian's struggle is not primarily against human opponents but against spiritual forces of evil. It isn't just a feeling, emotions, heaviness, or weak flesh that oppress us; evil spirits are persons without a body but with a mission to separate us from God. If Jesus Himself could be a target of the devil, we mere mortals are in peril and must call on Him, God, and the Holy Spirit, for deliverance from sin and evil.

Is the Bible also God's warning to us about the devil's plot? From the Garden of Eden in Genesis to the final battle in Revelation, the devil and his demonic forces have relentlessly sought to separate humanity from God, the One who created us in His image, breathed life into us, and numbered our days. This is not a metaphorical struggle; it is a spiritual war that continues to rage. Even if you choose to stand with God, the enemy will bring the fight to you and your family with ruthless determination. And you will always fail if you try to solve your sin problems through a worldly lens. The flesh is weak.

The writing of this book and our podcast is a convergence of a chain of remarkable events.

On New Year's Eve 2022, my wife and I spent the evening with friends we'd long admired but never truly connected with, Loren Senior, a dad from our son's Little League circle, and his wife Amy. We felt honored to be invited.

Over conversation, we shared New Year's resolutions, something I've always taken seriously, writing them down and aiming to activate real change each year in both business and life. Loren asked if I'd like to hike with him in the new year. I enjoyed hiking, but, like most, I said yes to be amicable. This time, I was determined to be different; if I said "yes" to anything, I'd do it 100%. That night, we also discussed launching a regular men's fellowship coffee group, no agenda on religion or politics, simply "come as you are." Now, several years later, the group has met every single week, building great relationships. From that group, Greg Geenen, Loren, and I launched our Bonded Voices[7] podcast and built deep, lasting friendships with men I now love as brothers, men who were once just acquaintances.

Blynn Jennings, another baseball dad, invited me to his Tuesday night men's Bible study. It was February 2023. True to my resolution to follow through when I said yes, I walked into a church with 500 Christian men. As the band led worship, I was amongst charismatic worshippers. It was a group of spirit-filled men worshipping Jesus, and it was powerful. With my background in the Catholic church, this was a kind of experience I had rarely encountered

---

[7] www.bondedvoices.com

before, even in non-denominational churches in America. After the service, I noticed a sign near the back of the room, they were looking for people to serve on the worship team. With my background in the music industry, I saw this as an opportunity to discuss the sound. There, I met Galen, who oversaw the entire production.

Driving the following week, listening to talk radio, I heard on Seth Leibsohn's show a passing quote that I didn't hear who it was attributed to, something paraphrased along the lines of "The devil wanted to make the world so noisy that man could not hear the voice of God." It resonated so powerfully with me. After researching it at home, I found it was a C. S. Lewis paraphrase from his book, *The Screwtape Letters*. I love listening to audiobooks and found a version with John Cleese from Monty Python narrating. I was always perplexed by its description as "satire," that didn't sit well with me. Instead, it struck me as a roadmap to fight against the demonic forces that ruin lives with lies and deceit. I thought it could be an amazing self-help book for Christians if these ideas could be unpacked.

I set out to do a podcast on the spiritual warfare explained in this amazing book, *The Screwtape Letters*. I wanted to use the wisdom of C. S. Lewis to help Christians in their walk with God and fight back against the demonic forces, but I needed a co-host with a résumé of deep Bible study. My first choice was to ask Galen, fully expecting him to say no. Instead, his response was, "I'd love to!" We decided to give the first episode a test flight after services on a Sunday. So, with a little digital recorder, we recorded our first episode and birthed the podcast, *The Screwtape Letters Podcast: Confronting Evil in Our Time*. Its mission was to illuminate the challenge that the devil and his minions play in our world today to separate us from God so we can expose them, reject them, and put Jesus at the center of our lives.

We started our podcast in early 2024 and now have a listenership for our ministry on every continent. We didn't exactly know where this would lead us, we just felt guided. We prayed our way through our recordings, asking God to guide us through the process for whoever may listen. www.screwtapeletterspodcast.com

We were both acutely aware of the responsibility we had undertaken in dissecting C. S. Lewis's profound work. We were struck by how relevant it still is. Lewis wrote this over 80 years ago, yet the tactics Screwtape describes are as fresh as ever. I believe C. S. Lewis was uniquely anointed to write *The Screwtape Letters*. The complexity and depth of thought, phrasing, word choice, and subtlety can be lost unless you read each letter several times; there is so much to be unpacked.

In his preface, on July 5, 1941, at Magdalen College, C. S. Lewis wrote, "I have no intention of explaining how the correspondence which I now offer to the public fell into my hands. There are two equal and opposite errors into which our race can fall about the Devils. One is to disbelieve in their existence. The other is to believe and to fear an excessive and unhealthy interest in them. They themselves are equally pleased by both errors.

After reading our commentary on these letters, we hope it helps you reflect on how demonic strategies may be negatively influencing your life. The presence of temptation doesn't excuse sin, even if God has extended grace to you; He still sits in judgment, and His wrath and vengeance await us all. God has granted you free will and the power to choose differently. Yet through Jesus Christ, and the Holy Spirit's strength, you can walk in self-control and freedom.

Thank you for engaging with this book and our podcast. We hope our journey can be of help to you. Stand firm against the attacks of the enemy, so you can live a fuller, more Christ-centered life.

All truth is God's truth.

Ian's Story of Faith

My faith journey and relationship with Jesus Christ commenced at an early age. Raised in a Catholic family during the 1970s, we attended church services intermittently at St. John Fisher parish in Wyken, Coventry. Father Tarbuck was known for his stern demeanor. The congregation at the church formed a close-knit community, typical of English churches at that time. I briefly served as an altar boy and was actively involved during my Catholic confirmation, choosing the name Peter to signify my desire to be the "rock," a steadfast support for others.

On my mother's side of the family, my grandfather, one of 11 children and of Catholic Irish descent, married a Protestant woman. As a result, his family severed ties with him. The senselessness of sectarian violence in Northern Ireland and the UK puzzled me. Differences between Protestants and Catholics deserve a healthy debate, not violence or hatred. It's one thing for Christians to rally and war against evils like Communism or Nazism, but I'm pretty sure the sectarian violence was more of the Devil's work than of God's favor.

On my father's side, I had an atheist grandfather who was an avowed Communist. On VE Day, while everyone in the street displayed Union Jack flags outside their houses, he chose to fly the Hammer and Sickle. Despite being married to him, she had a profound relationship with Jesus and was a devout Catholic woman, whom I remember as the kindest person I have ever met and who played a crucial role in shaping my faith during my childhood. My grandmother demonstrated what it meant to have a relationship with Jesus Christ, attend church, connect with the community, honor the church organization, and show charity to the poor, despite our own economic hardships. Her influence was profound, and upon her passing, I honored her memory by at her wake, placing a picture of her with her exceptionally kind smile and the words "Amazing Grace" beneath it. Few people truly embody such a tribute, but she certainly did.

Like many baby boomers, my parents were going through a divorce, and my three brothers and I found ourselves caught in the middle. Father Tarbuck and St. John Fisher excommunicated my mother rather nastily with little compassion. This didn't rattle my faith as a child, but it did raise questions about organized religion. I know faith was a huge challenge for my mother during this period as divorced women were not looked upon kindly in that era. Why, all of a sudden, were we seeing so many families breaking down and so many school-aged children having out-of-wedlock babies? This didn't feel like the victory one would expect post WWII. Catholic and Protestant schools provided a Christian education and regular church attendance, but they were not able to stem the tide in society. Greater forces were in play.

My aunt on my father's side had become a nun before falling in love with a Catholic priest, and scandal broke out, forcing them to leave their ministry and emigrate to New Zealand, about as far away from Coventry as possible. The vow of chastity for priests, which is a heavy burden to bear for any man to not yield and love a family, wife, and children, and enjoy a healthy sex life, appears to go against God's command in Genesis, "And you, be fruitful and multiply." I also know the Catholic obsession around sex had a negative influence on me, which is a whole other conversation for another time.

It was the 80s, and times were tough in England with high unemployment and globalism on the rise. My faith relationship with Jesus Christ is what helped me through times of chaos, a divorced household, economic hardship, societal violence, and dark secular pressures.

My time spent living in America has found me prodigal at times, lured by worldly things that offer instant pleasure, yet I never lost my faith and by the grace of God, He found me and put me on his shoulders, He is that good. I have been blessed to know that I always had God to talk to, to listen to my prayers, concerns, and wants, and yes, He talks back to me.

I live a blessed life and have been married to my wife Allison for close to 25 years and have two wonderful children, Oliver and Winston.

Galen's Story of Faith

My childhood and upbringing were marked with simplicity and innocence. I grew up in a small town where things were happy and quaint. It was a place where a boy could grow up the all-American way; climbing trees, building forts, fishing, playing Little League Baseball. I enjoyed my favorite annual events like white Christmases, vacationing in Ocean City, Maryland, and watching the Yankees win the World Series. For me, things were as they should be. My faith was sort of the same way. I grew up going to church and had sincere faith from an early age. Looking back, I believe I was given the gift of a simple, childlike faith, something the Lord continued to grow and strengthen over time.

After high school, I went through what I'd call a passive prodigal season. When you become an adult, there's also a moment when you have to decide whether what you believe is truly yours or just something you were handed. I've come to believe that moment isn't a one-time event, it's a continual decision. The call, as Joshua 24:15 says, to "choose this day whom you will serve" is a daily one. But that early adult season of life is particularly crucial. And for me, it was the first time I had to ask myself whether I believed what I believed because it was real and true or simply because I grew up around it. God used that question to draw me into something deeper.

While I never completely abandoned God, I did gradually neglect my faith and spiritual life. Life was happening, and I wasn't actively pursuing the Lord the way a young man should. That began to change when I was about 20 years old. God brought good people into my life, one in particular, who was intentional about challenging me and encouraging me to be more serious about my relationship with the Lord. This became a season of spiritual reactivation. I became very active in my church and threw myself into Scripture, theology, apologetics, sermons, and books, everything I could get my hands on. That season wasn't rebellion that needed correcting, as much as it was passivity that needed reawakening. God was good to allow it.

Within a few years, I felt a strong, clear call to serve the Lord in a formal way, and I enrolled in Bible college. I'd never intended to pursue ministry. I didn't grow up wanting to be a pastor and had no idea what that road would even look like. But I knew God was calling me to something. I already had a few years of college under my belt, and this time around, I took it more seriously. I was older. I was paying for it myself. I was ready. And I'm incredibly grateful for the theological and spiritual foundation that was laid during those years and to the great men who poured into me.

After Bible college, I moved to New York City to serve at a church and a Christian nonprofit in Manhattan. It was a unique ministry that combined church planting, food distribution, and practical service. We operated a large private food pantry that distributed roughly $4–5 million in food each year to our local community. I spent my days studying, teaching Bible studies, leading mission teams, and loading many banana boxes onto and off of a van all over NYC. It was a season when I went to bed tired every night, knowing I had poured out everything I had. I saw the fruit of that labor in real time. And like my childhood, times were good.

That time in New York also led me through very challenging times. As a young and somewhat naive guy, I faced an Enemy that up to that point I had only known of in theory. Scripture speaks of spiritual powers and principalities, of demonic forces, often assigned to regions. And if the world is a spiritual battlefield, which it is, cities often function like the Enemy's headquarters. The city is the heartbeat of every worldly economy, both good and bad; people go to make it "big," to be seen, and to escape. It's a system Satan knows how to exploit. I understood that, in theory, but I didn't fully understand it until I found myself in the crosshairs. During those years in NYC, I'm convinced we battled the spirit of Jezebel in a very real way. It was a prolonged season of adversity and spiritual warfare that affected me, the staff, and the ministry. It left me bruised, discouraged, and, for a time, jaded.

But the Lord orchestrates all things for good, and He gave me a silver lining in that season: I met my wife. In what was the darkest time, He brought blessing. After a season of dating, I moved to Arizona, where she was finishing her studies. I stayed connected to the church in New York from afar, but it felt like my ministry was coming to an end. At the time, I thought my pastoral journey was complete and over. And I had a peace about it.

But in time, I went on staff at a church in Arizona, became a pastor again, and quickly realized that the difficulty, adversity, and warfare I had gone through in New York were exactly what helped me to serve in a new season. It's true what they say: your test becomes your testimony. Your trial becomes your credential. Ministry in Arizona was fruitful, stretching, and filled with purpose. It was during that time that I met Ian.

With his background in music and media, he offered to serve in worship and production, and we immediately connected and became fast friends. At one point, the church was going through a teaching series on Elijah, and the subject of spiritual warfare came up again and again. As we shared stories and reflected on our own experiences, Ian suggested we do something together, something grounded in Lewis's

The Screwtape Letters, one of the most profound Christian works on spiritual warfare.

This book is the next step. I'm not any more qualified than most to offer commentary on a classic Christian work or unpack the tactics of Satan in the world today. But my story is one of a naive faithful who, by God's grace, has been through intense spiritual warfare and has seen firsthand that the Lord fights for us. Satan's plan is to do anything he can to pull us off course, steal, kill, and destroy. But the battle belongs to the Lord. Once you've seen the spiritual realm for what it truly is, you can't unsee it. And you wouldn't want to. The Enemy is real. The warfare is real. And Jesus is greater.